The Politics
of Civil Service Reform

Teaching Texts in Law and Politics

David A. Schultz
General Editor

Vol. 1

PETER LANG
New York • Washington, D.C./Baltimore • Boston
Bern • Frankfurt am Main • Berlin • Vienna • Paris

David A. Schultz
& Robert Maranto

The Politics
of Civil Service Reform

PETER LANG
New York • Washington, D.C./Baltimore • Boston
Bern • Frankfurt am Main • Berlin • Vienna • Paris

Library of Congress Cataloging-in-Publication Data

Schultz, David A.
The politics of civil service reform / David A. Schultz & Robert Maranto.
p. cm. — (Teaching texts in law and politics ; v. 1)
Includes bibliographical references and index.
1. Civil service—United States—History. 2. Civil service reform—
United States—History. I. Maranto, Robert. II. Title. III. Series.
JK681.S38   353.004—dc20   96-24399
ISBN 0-8204-3379-9
ISSN 1083-3447

Die Deutsche Bibliothek-CIP-Einheitsaufnahme

Schultz, David A.:
The politics of civil service reform / David A. Schultz & Robert Maranto.
–New York; Washington, D.C./Baltimore; Boston; Bern;
Frankfurt am Main; Berlin; Vienna; Paris: Lang.
(Teaching texts in law and politics; Vol. 1)
ISBN 0-8204-3379-9
NE: Maranto, Robert:; GT

Cover design by James F. Brisson.

The paper in this book meets the guidelines for permanence and durability
of the Committee on Production Guidelines for Book Longevity
of the Council of Library Resources.

© 1998 Peter Lang Publishing, Inc., New York

Printed in the United States of America.

To my father, who taught me the value and dignity
of public service.
—DS

To my wife, April W. Gresham, for all her help, and to my father
Anthony Joseph Maranto, who introduced me to this topic during
his thirty-five years of faithful federal service.
—RM

Acknowledgments

There are many individuals whom we would like to thank and acknowledge as helpful in our efforts to write this book.

From David, warm thanks go to Brian Porto, Kent Rismiller, L. Tucker Gibson, Chris Smith, and a host of other individuals at various regional political-science conventions who heard portions of the chapters that compose this book and who offered wonderful comments and suggestions.

From Robert, thanks go to Eric M. Uslaner, Charles Walcott, David Fitch, Kay Knickrehm, and James P. Pfiffner for teaching me about government in general and academia in particular. I wish to thank Paul P. Van Riper, whose classic *History of the United States Civil Service* taught me that very little is really new. For their encouraging comments on earlier drafts, I wish to thank Larry Beer and Marissa Martino Golden. For her infinite patience and devoted fact-checking, I wish to thank my wife, April W. Gresham. The greatest thanks must go to my fellow federal workers, who never ceased to surprise me with their analytic ability, flexibility, good humor, and real patriotism. First among these, I wish to thank my first and best teacher, Anthony Joseph Maranto, who stimulated my interest in the civil service during his thirty-five years of faithful federal service.

Contents

Chapter I

American Bureaucracy and the Politics of Civil Service Reform

> *In the United States it has long been popular first to denounce
> 'bureaucracy' and then to augment it. Our inability to live
> entirely happily either with or without a complex administrative
> arm of the national state is only a modern reaction to an ancient
> dilemma. The relation of citizen to public official, governed to
> governor, has always posed a central problem of politics
> whatever the form or theory of government. When in a demo-
> cracy the magistrate is declared to be both master and servant,
> the difficulties are only compounded.[1]*

Images of the Federal Bureaucracy in American Political Culture

Americans view government in attitudes that range from
indifference to hate. Be it the fear of big government that derailed
President Clinton's efforts in 1994 to reform health care, distrust
vented toward the Bureau of Alcohol, Tobacco, and Firearms for its
violent standoff at Waco, Texas, and Ruby Ridge, Montana, or
demands to limit the power of the Internal Revenue Service, public
opinion in the United States demonstrates that despite a desire for
government services, no one appears too willing to trust the federal
government and bureaucracy.

In popular depictions, the terms "civil servant," "bureaucrat,"
and "bureaucracy" cast quite negative images. All too often these are
derisive terms suggesting to many people bloated, faceless, inefficient
organizations that are intrusive, powerful, and out of control.
Bureaucrats are pictured as inept, unproductive, and unwilling to

work. They are people who come to work late, drink coffee and socialize all day, and then go home early. These stereotypes are capped off by the belief that civil service laws protect lazy workers and prevent them from ever being fired. Charles Goodsell aptly stated about civil servants:

> ...[T]he organs of mass culture usually depict them, as some-
> what contradictorily, as lazy and incompetent on the one hand
> and malicious and aggrandizing on the other. In other words, we
> are supposed to consider them both passively inadequate and
> actively malevolent.[2]

Depictions of the federal bureaucracy are now so negative that presidential candidates, even those with long-term federal service, run as Washington outsiders. They promise to "reinvent government" by reforming it through the elimination of programs or by turning over to the states many of the basic services that had previously been performed by the federal government. The assumption is that the states, being closer and more in touch with the people, will be able to better administer programs than a distant, detached federal government.

Yet negative depictions of bureaucrats and the fear of the federal government are not of recent invention. Over 160 years ago, in language reminiscent of President Reagan when he first took office in 1981, Andrew Jackson criticized the federal government as being full of individuals politically indifferent to his political agenda and the interests of the common man.[3] As a result, he initiated one of the first of many efforts to reinvent the federal government, seeking to make the bureaucracy more accountable to him by making its composition more representative of his class background and the political interests of his supporters.[4]

Thus, starting as early as the middle of the nineteenth century, what became known as the spoils system was born. The spoils system was meant to be a way for the president to increase his political and administrative control over the federal government. However, awarding of federal jobs by presidents to loyal supporters was soon described in the media (and among those who did not get jobs!) as a corrupt form of patronage that did not create an efficient competent federal service. It produced instead opportunities for scandal, private profiteering, and the corruption of the public interest.[5]

From the Civil War to 1912, Populists, Progressives, and other social reformers in politics and the media reiterated these criticisms of the federal bureaucracy and again described how corrupt and inefficient patronage was.[6] Stories and political cartoons in many newspapers again reinforced the image of the lazy incompetent bureaucrat. Thus, to clean up the government and make government more efficient and less political,[7] a merit civil service system was instituted to ensure that the most qualified individuals were hired for jobs in the government.

Presidential races in the late nineteenth and early twentieth century were concerned in varying degrees with the incompetence and corruption of the patronage system, and each president sought means to gain control over the ever-expanding federal bureaucracy. Demands and promises to extend the merit principle to more and more workers were made by practically every president through Truman. Finally, in the 1960s and 1970s, with the rapid growth of the federal government, popular accounts of the government depicted a large, bloated organization out of control. Demands were again made to reform the federal government, to make it more efficient, less political, and more responsive to the popular will. Hence, while today we rail against big government and the power of the federal bureaucracy, such attacks are not new but seem entrenched in the fabric of American political discourse.

Along with popular-culture depictions of the bureaucracy is been the academic community's equally negative view of the bureaucracy or bureaucratic reform. Charles Goodsell notes that academics usually denounce bureaucracies and bureaucrats as "dysfunctional" in a variety of ways.[8] Economists describe bureaucracies as inefficient, unproductive, or monopolistic. Some sociologists describe them as power driven, while others see bureaucrats as part of a decision-making structure that reproduces hierarchies of inequality. Even many introductory American politics textbooks reinforce these attitudes by keying in on bureaucratic red tape, the difficulty of firing a federal employee, or "bureaucratese," (the distorted and complicated prose often used in government).[9]

Overall, popular and academic views of bureaucrats and the civil service create the impression that serious reform is essential. How accurate are these images?[10] In part, this book addresses this question by providing a history of the politics of civil service reform.

Why Study Civil Service Reform?

Despite extensive media coverage of the federal government, usually in terms of what it has done wrong and not right, there is a general ignorance about what the civil service system is and how it operates within our political system. Few introductory American politics textbooks spend much time discussing the civil service system, instead keying in on the "pathologies" of American bureaucratic structures.[11] The perception that civil service reform and the federal bureaucracy are boring topics, and the lack of an accessible text on these subjects, also contribute to a neglect of this topic and confusion about how the civil service system operates.

This ignorance often leads to a misunderstanding of how and in what ways the federal bureaucracy is an enormously powerful institution in American politics. The federal government has numerous agencies that have the power to regulate the environment (Environmental Protection Agency), workplace safety (Occupational Safety and Health Agency), airline safety (Federal Aviation Administration Agency), and the food and drug industry (Food and Drug Administration). The civil service is also involved with the regulation of the supply of money in our economy (Federal Reserve Board), and in administering programs that supply welfare, housing, and food to the poor (Housing and Urban Development or HUD, and Health and Human Services or HHS). Even with recent efforts to scale back federal programs, civil servants within the federal bureaucracy remain powerful and important forces within the United States, and they shall remain powerful so long the public continues to demand new regulations to protect them against some new risk or problem that they have confronted.

In looking at the power of the federal civil service, it is important to know how large it is. In 1996, there were over 2,500,000 civilian employees in the federal government,[12] of which over ninety percent were covered by civil service laws. In contrast, there are over three million state and ten million local public employees in the United States. With the vast majority of federal employees at all levels of employment covered by civil service laws, it is obvious that these workers have enormous influence in the federal bureaucracy. They are important in making policy, enforcing laws, providing public information, working with Congress, and in performing hundreds of other important functions. The civil service system, then, is an important institution within the federal government. Given the size and strength of the federal civil service, it is no wonder that while many presidents start off seeking to change the government, the bureaucracy in the end "captures" the president, forcing the latter to alter or compromise his agenda. Thus, to understand how the civil service system works and how it evolved gives students of American government a better understanding of how our American political system operates.

Hence, understanding the structure and role of the civil service within the federal bureaucracy sheds some light on the forces that constrain presidents in office. As noted above, recent presidents have run against the bureaucracy and sought to reform it only to find, as we shall see below, much difficulty in securing that goal. Many presidents have come to office with a political agenda and were frustrated both by the slowness of the bureaucracy and by their inability to remove career civil servants who they perceived were antagonistic to their goals. For example, President Reagan came to office with a huge electorial victory and clear political programs but found few vacancies in the federal bureaucracy to fill with his supporters. He found the civil service system a check upon his power.

In addition to the presidential-bureaucratic conflict, the topic of civil service reform clearly touches upon an American concern with political corruption that dates back to our founding. There is an ever-present fear in American politics that government or its workers are corrupt, and that the best way to control both is either to limit the size of the government or, as a last resort, to keep the government but place significant limitations upon its powers. Some wish to make the bureaucracy subject to political checks similar to those that apply to the major branches of the national government. In short, civil service reform strikes at the heart of America's desire for a clean, but efficient and limited power.

Finally, a history of the politics of civil service demonstrates numerous alternative models of how we have organized the federal government and the national governmental apparatus.[13] In the past, the spoils system and the civil service merit system, among other models, have been employed as means to organize the government and a knowledge of these systems is valuable for comparison to current means of staffing the federal service. Additionally, as will be described below, discussion of the politics of civil service reform show how over time different goals have guided how we have wanted our bureaucracy and government to be organized.

For example, do we wish to create a national government and federal service premised upon spoils and patronage where political loyalty determines the composition of the federal staff and where turn-over of personnel is significant after every election? Or do we wish to create a more professional federal service premised less upon political loyalty and more upon personal competence? In many ways, this choice is not simply a matter of personnel administration, but it also implicates significant questions about the very structure of our political system in terms of the relationship between party politics, elections, and governance. As this book will show, past reforms and political conflicts among the president, Congress, and the courts to define the structure and values of the federal service clearly have had an influence on the present organization of our political system, and a study of civil service reform will show that there is nothing new about the debates surrounding current reform demands.

The Purpose, Goals, and Organization of This Book

This book provides a short concise analysis of the politics of civil service reform in the United States. It examines the changes in the structure and organization of the federal service within the context of changing ideologies or concepts of public administration, as well as within the context of competing efforts by the president, Congress, and the courts to influence and control the federal bureaucracy. Civil service reform in the United States is examined by showing how the different goals and strategies have been implemented to make the federal bureaucracy and employees either more efficient or more accountable to the president, Congress, the public, or to its constituents.

Our approach is mainly "neoinstitutional," concerned with "a set of rules about how administrative agencies should be organized and managed" and on how individuals who work in those organizations should also be organized and managed.[14] We also examine these organizational rules within an ever-changing political environment to show how there has not been one, but numerous attempts to organize the federal bureaucracy and the federal government to achieve a variety of goals or management practices.

One goal will be to discuss this neoinstitutional and historical approach mainly with reference to recent presidential reforms and show how their efforts are similar to past reform efforts. In part, we book will also address presidential or presidential appointee interaction with the civil service (less than congressional and judicial conflicts) because our concern is to concentrate more on the executive department conflicts in bureaucratic reform than on the separation of powers issues or conflicts between the civil service and the courts or the Congress.

By primarily examining the executive branch, this book keys in on the role of presidential leadership in the executive branch and draws out the conflicts between the president and the civil service. By focusing on the role of the president as providing American bureaucratic and political leadership, the intention is to explain the evolution of the normative questions concerning the scope and proper role of presidential control over the bureaucracy. We will try to show that clashes between the president and the federal bureaucracy are more complex than previously thought, and that it is important to understand these clashes if one wishes to comprehend presidential power and the organization of the federal government.

Four Goals of Civil Service Reform

For the most part, this book will place the politics of civil service reform within the context of attempts to reconcile four basic goals. These goals are: 1) to use the bureaucracy as a source of presidential patronage; 2) to promote neutral competence and rational, efficient administration of the law and government programs; 3) to give the president greater political control over the bureaucracy; and 4) to reconcile bureaucratic organization with the large (constitutional) goals of Madisonian democracy and American politics,; i.e., to create politically accountable public servants, subject to checks and balances, congressional and judicial oversight, and with sharp limits on their political power.

All four of these goals were important or stressed at various times in American bureaucratic reform, with occasionally the four goals operating at cross purposes. We simultaneously and perhaps contradictorily expect that presidents will use the bureaucracy as a source of patronage, that they will have political control over the bureaucracy, and that bureaucrats will also be politically neutral and competent, and thus beyond the control of presidential abuse while also accountable to Congress, the courts, and the American public.

A preliminary review of these four goals provides clarification not only of what they mean, but also a summary of the way much of this book is organized.

Presidential Political and Administrative Control

The president is the only person in the United States who is voted for and elected (although indirectly through the electoral college) by all of the people. This makes the presidency the only truly national office in this country, and perhaps only the president can claim to be the spokesman or the political or national representative of the interests of the people. When presidential candidates make certain campaign promises, such as to lower taxes or increase spending on social programs, presidents often claim that they have been elected by the people to live up to their promises and to try to make them into policies or laws. In the words of politics, they have a mandate for their programs.

Article II, section 1, of the U.S. Constitution states that the "executive Power shall be vested in a President of the United States of America." Constitutional text appears to make the president the chief administrator or head of executive branch and bureaucracy with powers similar to those we would give to a chief executive officer (CEO) of a major private business or corporation. A president can claim to be both the political leader of America and the chief administrator of the federal bureaucracy with complete control over the executive branch. This suggests that there should not be any internal limits upon how the president decides to organize the federal bureaucracy, or whom he decides to hire or fire. The principle of separation of powers, and the investing in him of the executive power, prevents other branches of government from interfering in the way he organizes the federal bureaucracy. Any attempts to try to limit his control would be to deny him either his constitutionally granted powers or his political mandate to implement the promises and policies he was elected to secure.

Presidents since Washington have tried to make the claim for nearly absolute control over the executive branch such that there should not be limits upon appointment or removal power, or upon the intrusion of other branches to investigate alleged criminal activities within the executive branch. While this claim has been made, Congress and the courts have not always agreed and have upheld some limitations.[15] Additionally, Congress, in seeking to control the federal bureaucracy to secure its legislative mandates, often disagrees with the belief that the president has sole control over the federal government. As a result, Congress and the president often conflict and disagree over who shall control the federal bureaucracy and for what purposes. Throw into that conflict judicial oversight of the rights of federal workers, or the scope of Congress or the president to act, as well as the organizational interests of the federal bureaucracy itself, and the final result is a politicized conflict to chart the course of the federal bureaucracy.

Bureaucracy as a Source of Patronage

One use that the federal bureaucracy has provided is a source of jobs for loyal supporters or friends of the President. Though presidents as early as Washington and Jefferson gave jobs to supporters and those who shared their political beliefs, it was not until President Andrew Jackson in 1829 that filling the federal bureaucracy with friends, cronies, and supporters became prevalent. In part this was because there were very few federal jobs to award under the first few presidents due to the small size of the federal bureaucracy.[16] But also it was not an accepted practice to use the bureaucracy as a source of patronage in the early years of the American government.

But with President Jackson and, more particularly, with Lincoln, the cry "to the victor belong the spoils" signaled that the federal government was a way to reward friends and supporters with jobs and to bring in voters on election day. That practice continued beyond those presidents. Even today, many of the appointments to the Cabinet, to higher level administrative positions, and to ambassadorships go not to career federal employees but to friends, contributors, and supporters as a form of reward.

The appointment process and organization of the federal government from Washington to John Quincy Adams will be discussed in chapter two, while the rise of the spoils system under Jackson and Lincoln will be discussed in chapter three.

Neutral Competence

One complaint lodged against the spoils system in the nineteenth century, and which continues to be levied even today, is that using the federal bureaucracy as a source of patronage politicizes the bureaucracy and renders it both ethically corrupt and administratively inefficient. Individuals who get jobs simply because they are friends or supporters of the president may not be the most qualified. Some jobs may require technical expertise or skill and friends appointed without regard to qualifications or the requirements of the job may be inefficient or incompetent. They may simply lack the skills that are needed for that job.

If political friends are appointed, the operations of the bureaucracy could become very political and unstable. If a new president were completely free to replace all federal employees, then the running of the government would perhaps become very inefficient, unorganized, and unstable owing to the large turnovers in personnel. If political loyalty were the only reason why individuals received jobs, the enforcement of laws and the administration of programs might be perceived as political, thus undermining the public support and legitimacy for the government. Some appointees might enforce the law or award programs to friends, loyalists, or party members. Also, if all the positions were left open to presidential appointment, federal workers might be pressured to donate to the political causes of the president or be forced to work on his campaign.

Fears that unregulated patronage or a spoils system would be politically corrupt or administratively inefficient led to numerous reforms, starting with the Pendleton Act in 1883. The Pendleton Act was the first attempt at creating a civil service system in America through which individuals would receive their jobs not on the basis of political connections but upon a merit principle. Individuals would have to take some type of test to prove that they were qualified for the job. Once they received that job, moreover, they were supposed to be secure in their position and protected from arbitrary dismissal.

The early purpose of the merit system was both to ensure that qualified candidates were hired and that these candidates would be immune from political pressures. Subsequent developments in civil service law, along with presidential prerogatives, placed more workers under its protections. Administrative reorganizations sought to make the workflow in the bureaucracy more efficient and the workers more productive. Subsequent laws and court rulings were also meant to guarantee that federal employees were politically neutral, beyond presidential manipulation, and technically competent in the work they were doing. This idea is known as neutral competence. Hence, while efficiency is one reason to enforce neutral competence in the federal bureaucracy, congressional fear that the president would use federal workers to serve his political preferences, or presidential fears that federal workers would pursue political objectives at odds with his desires, led to efforts to politically neutralize the federal service.

The rise of the merit system, the Pendleton Act, and the move to make the federal bureaucracy efficient are discussed in chapters four and five, with chapter five discussing the extension of the civil service system under several presidents. The remaining chapters discuss changes in the civil service system under Carter, Reagan, Bush, and Clinton.

Bureaucratic Power and Madisonian Democracy

When the American Constitution was written in 1787, three basic goals influenced the Founding Fathers' thinking. These goals were to preserve individual liberty, promote republican or popularly elected and accountable government, and place limits upon factions or groups of individuals who might pursue their own private interests to the destruction of the public interest or the interests or liberties of others.[17] To secure these goals, the Founders wrote a constitution that embodied several principles to organize the new national government. Among the most important are separation of powers and checks and balances, both of which were viewed as important to limiting the political power of the different branches of government.

Separation of powers is the principle that each branch of the national government—the executive, the legislative, and the judicial—should have distinct powers.[18] The purpose of separating the different branches of government with distinct functions was to prevent any one branch from possessing too much power. According to James Madison in *Federalist # 51*, should any one of the branches become too powerful it would be able to threaten the other branches of government or the liberty of the citizens. Separation of powers was a way to limit the power of any one branch of government.

However, while Madison endorsed separation of powers, in *Federalist # 48* he also argued that the different branches of government should not be so separate that they would have nothing to do with one another. While each branch should have security against the invasion by another branch, there should also be some sharing or mixing of power among the different branches of government so that each branch could serve as a check or be a balance upon the power of another branch. The principle of checks and balances along with separation of powers were two organizing principles of the national government that sought to prevent the concentration of too much political power in the hands of one branch of government. The goal was to prevent tyranny and any faction from dominating any one branch of the government, or to prevent any one branch of government from dominating another.[19]

In constructing a national government organized according to these political principles, the first three articles of the Constitution dealt with the power of Congress, the presidency, and the federal courts respectively. Surprisingly, the Constitution is silent not only on the method of appointment and removal of federal executive officers and employees, but it is silent even in terms of the very structure and organization of the federal bureaucracy.[20]

The Constitution does not mention the federal bureaucracy or the civil service, and one of the most important problems facing the organization of the federal government was how to reconcile the power of unelected and often tenured-for-life civil servants with the overall goals of Madisonian democracy that included checks and balances, separation of powers, and representative (elected) government.[21] Various means have been suggested to constitutionalize the federal bureaucracy and make it more politically accountable to either the president, Congress, or perhaps even the people directly. These methods include numerous federal court administrative law decisions and the passage of numerous laws, such as the Administrative Procedures Act (APA) in 1946, to open up the decision-making process of the federal bureaucracy. While many critics disagree over how successful such reforms have been, it is sufficient to say that one goal of bureaucratic reform has been to make it more representative of important political interests by integrating them into the bargaining process of the American political system.[22]

Attempts to open up the federal bureaucracy to more political control, especially to the president and to a lesser extent Congress, will be a theme that weaves in and out of most of the chapters of this book. In chapter five efforts to reconcile bureaucratic power with political power will be discussed by examining the conflict between the career civil service and presidential policy-making. However, throughout the book, one theme that should be understood is that civil service reform is one of several ways to constrain and control political power.

Thus, the four goals of presidential control, spoils, neutral competence, and political accountability are in a tension. There are significant normative questions regarding how political we want the bureaucracy to be without sacrificing its administrative neutrality or competence, and there is also a limit to how much control the president or Congress should have over the bureaucracy without threatening it with political manipulation. In reconciling these goals, tradeoffs may need to be made in terms of political neutrality versus responsiveness, or efficiency versus effectiveness, or in patronage versus merit, with the different tradeoffs carrying with them different pluses and minuses.[23] This book will show how at different eras in American history each of these different concepts or goals have influenced how the federal bureaucracy has been organized.

In sum, we will show that organizing the federal government though a merit service system is one of several rival ways to organize the federal government to reconcile the cited four goals.

Bureaucratic Organization and Power

Before concluding this introduction, a brief discussion of what a bureaucracy is and how bureaucracies are generally organized is essential to understanding the problems surrounding civil service and bureaucratic reform.

Max Weber, a famous early-twentieth-century German sociologist, wrote an important essay on bureaucracies and bureaucratic organization.[24] According to Weber, modern society, organizations, and, for our purposes, the federal government, are organized according to a rational-legal authority which is best depicted as a large pyramid with the president at the apex and various levels of workers found at different levels in the pyramid. According to the Weberian model of bureaucratic power, there are several basic characteristics that can be found in this type of pyramid structure:

♦   Authority, power, and knowledge are hierarchial with those higher up in the pyramid having more authority, and such, than those lower on the pyramid.

♦   Bureaucratic organization is marked by clear lines of authority, divisions of labor, and a movement of decision-making from the top to the bottom of the pyramid.

♦   Bureaucratic decision-making and action is marked by the regularization of procedures and the following of specified rules and habits.

♦   The power of a bureaucracy rests upon the special knowledge and expertise of its officeholders, and upon its ability to issue sanctions or rewards in the enforcement of its rules and procedures.

Weber contended that employees in a bureaucracy would have to prove fitness for employment or promotion through meeting certain qualifications, and generally an employee would receive life tenure or security for her job once she was hired. In sum, we may describe a bureaucracy as a way of structuring a group of people to achieve specified goals. It is characterized by specific organizing principles, namely specialization of function, action according to fixed rules, and a hierarchial, or chain of command, authority structure, with power concentrated at the top of the pyramid. In a simple hierarchy, people are organized into ranks, with each rank superior to the one below it. A bureaucracy is typically divided into subunits based on a division-of-labor principle in which people hired for their specialized skills accomplish specified tasks or functions. Coordination and control of subunits and employees are based largely on the orders of superiors within the hierarchy.[25]

While in this book we will generally describe the federal bureaucracy as one organization, and bureaucrats as if they were all the same, there are clearly differences. The federal bureaucracy is composed of thousands of different departments, agencies, and subagencies, each with its own particular missions, goals, and organizational structures. Some organizations have missions related to the military or the national defense, others to domestic policy, others to enforcing the law, others for any of a thousand other purposes. Depending on the age of the bureaucracy, its mission, and it's members, among other things, different bureaucracies may be quite distinct from one another.[26]

Not all employees in the federal bureaucracy are alike. They have many different personal goals, motivations, and objectives.[27] Differences in particular bureaucracies and bureaucrats are important, but they will be passed over here because such distinctions are not crucial to the general history of civil service reform.

Notes

1. Paul P. Van Riper 1958: p. 1.

2. Goodsell 1985: p. 104.

3. Van Riper 1958: pp. 32-33; Pessen 1978: pp. 313-316.

4. Pessen 1978: p. 314.

5. Van Riper 1958: p. 63, notes the criticisms of Jackson's patronage appointments by Clay, Calhoun, and Webster.

6. Van Riper 1958: pp. 74-95.

7. Van Riper 1958: p. 85.

8. Goodsell 1985: pp. 6-11.

9. Wilson 1986: pp. 368 and 371 offer two different study boxes on how to fire a bureaucrat, while on pp. 372-373, there are a discussion, two cartoons, and a study box on how to speak "bureaucratese." Harris 1986: p. 503 has a special study box on how to fire a bureaucrat.

10. Goodsell 1985: pp. 16-38, does examine some survey data of personal interaction with bureaucracies and finds that these impressions are different than general views of bureaucracies and bureaucrats.

11. Hinkley 1990: pp. 351-352; Patterson 1990: p. 520; Edwards, 1988: pp. 279-281, and Harris 1986: p. 500, all provide about one or two pages on the civil service system, or why it came about, or how it works. Edwards 1988: pp. 281-282, provides the best of the introductory textbook discussions on what he calls structural reform of the civil service system under Carter and Reagan.

12. Census Bureau 1989: p. 318.

13. Skrowronek 1982; Skocpol 1992.

14. Knott, and Miller 1987: p. 6.

15. For two examples of how the Supreme Court has limited presidential power by rejecting separation of powers claims compare, *U.S. v. Nixon*, 418 U.S. 683 (1974), and *Morrison v. Olson*, 487 U.S. 654 (1988).

16. For example, in 1816, there were only 4,837 civilian employees of which only 535 worked in Washington, D.C. Census Bureau 1971: p. 1101.

17. Madison 1937: *Federalist #10*.

18. Madison 1937: *Federalist # 47*.

19. Dahl 1965: pp. 32-33.

20. Rosenbloom 1971: p. 24.

21. Woll 1989: pp. 171-172, discusses the attempt to constitutionalize the federal bureaucracy by applying the principles of checks and balances and separation of powers to its operations.

22. Mosher 1982; Krislov and Rosenbloom 1981.

23. Ingraham 1995.

24. Originally, the essay on bureaucracy was part III, chapter 6, of his *Wirtschaft and Gesellschaft*, but it has been translated and reprinted as "Bureaucracy" in Gerth and Mills 1979: pp. 196-267.

25. Medeiros, and Schmitt 1977: pp. 1-2.

26. Downs 1986: describes in detail the numerous differences among bureaucracies or agencies.

27. Downs 1986: pp. 79-112.

Chapter II

Government by Gentlemen: Federal Service from Washington to Jackson

Creating a New Federal Government

The structure of the federal government and the federal service has changed dramatically over time. In 1789 when George Washington took over as the first president, there was no federal government to speak of. There were neither cabinet departments nor officers, nor even any rules describing how the federal government, employment, or service should be structured. The newly written and adopted Constitution was of little help. It did not discuss a federal service or the rules governing appointment, hiring, and firing of executive staff. All of this was left to Washington and the first Congress to define, leaving open many possible ways they could have chosen to organize the federal government and the people who work in it.

The organization of the American federal service has evolved through several distinct phases since Washington's nomination.[1] These different eras of American public administration are distinguished in part by the debate over the underlying political values influencing a president's administration and appointment strategy.[2] However, these different eras of public administration also reflect different ways the American national government and political structure are organized. They describe different ways political parties and partisan politics related to the government as well as how people were recruited for government service.[3] Hence, describing the federal service in terms of different eras also says a fair amount about the ethics, values, and political and governing system at any particular time in the United States.

American bureaucratic organization can be divided into six

eras that demonstrated personnel and management of the federal government have been structured. We call the first era the "Government by Gentlemen." Encompassing the period from George Washington's inauguration to the start of Jackson's presidency (1789-1829), this era was characterized by a relatively small federal government and civil service, with the latter appointed mostly from individuals with upper class backgrounds, sharing similar values.

The second era is the "Government by the Common Man," crossing the time from Jackson's presidency to the passage of the Pendleton Act (1829-1883). This was the high point of the spoils system, with political appointments determined by party and party loyalty.

The third era is the "Government by the Good," which started with the passage of the Pendleton Act (1883-1906). During this era, the first civil service reforms are implemented, motivated in part by ethical and moral concerns, as the federal government struggles with reforming and rooting out the spoils system.

The fourth era is the "Government by the Efficient," and it is marked by the creation of the New York Bureau of Municipal Research (1906-1937). During this period the impetus for civil service reform was less on the alleged immorality of spoils and more on its inefficiency, with reformers seeking to implement civil service reforms to make the federal government more efficient and business-like.

"Government by Managers" describes the fifth period, which begins with the report of the Brownlow Committee on presidential management and continues through the start of President Johnson's Great Society programs (1937-1968). During this era the scope and size of federal functions increases dramatically as a result of the New Deal, World War II, and the Great Society programs of the 1960s.

The sixth and presumably not the last era is the "Government by Social Workers," and it crosses the time from the Minnowbrook Conference on public administration (1968 to the present). During this period, public administration stressed issues beyond efficiency, including values such as justice and fairness in the implementation of federal programs. Emphasis on such values clearly reflected the social concerns of the time.

Arguably, since the 1980s a new era of public administration ethics has developed that could be described as "Government by Businessmen." This era stresses the importance of running government like a business, seeking efficiency, reduced government functions and budgets, and efforts to streamline regulation of business. Like the "Government by the Efficient," this new ethic places a premium on efficiency and the importance of management techniques in organizing the federal government, yet the "Government by Businessmen" is different in terms of its effort to limit regulatory activity, decrease the scope of governmental activity, and return power back to states and the private sector. Hence, it is an effort to make the federal government smaller and more efficient.

Overall, each time period represents a different way the operations of the federal government are organized. These eras also provide rough descriptions of how presidents filled appointments, the basic values shared by Congresses and the president in terms of how the federal government should be staffed, and who should be hired to staff it. While these different eras may not exactly describe all the characteristics and politics of each time period, they do provide a good label to describe the way different time periods, Congress, and presidents opted to organize and run the federal government.

Colonial American and Revolutionary War Influences on the Federal Service

Early history of the federal bureaucracy and administrative values of the "Government by Gentlemen" were influenced by the American Revolutionary War and American colonial experiences with England. Clashes with King George III led to an American fear of placing too much power in the hands of a strong executive or president. Generally, the first few presidents were given very little control over the federal government, with Congress asserting broad control.

The first few presidents also had little power in the new

government for three additional reasons. First, the Founders felt that Congress was to be the most powerful branch of the national government, with the president merely an administrator of congressional will. An indication of the relative weakness of the office of the presidency can be seen in the Constitution, where legislative power is amply spelled out in Article I, while executive power is briefly described in Article II. Congressional power included broad powers to regulate commerce, taxation, and declare war, and engage in some limited diplomatic and foreign policy activities.[4] Yet presidential power was limited in terms of the president's control over even the executive branch. In addition, executive power to make executive and judicial appointments was subject to approval by the Senate.

Second, while the Constitution appeared to give the national government broad powers, they were used sparingly by the national government through most of the eighteenth, nineteenth, and even early twentieth centuries. Because of the federal plan of the Founders, political power was to be divided between state and national governments, with the former given the responsibility to undertake most of the domestic activities and the national government most of the foreign policy functions.[5] Thus, in the early years of the American republic, there were few administrative duties for the national government to perform and little need for much of a federal bureaucracy.

Third, given that the federal government was limited in size, that meant that in the early years of the American republic, as compared to today, the president had few day-to-day duties to perform. Few duties meant that the presidency was fairly weak, and it also meant that the federal bureaucracy would be quite small by today's comparisons. During Washington's presidency there were only a few hundred federal employees, and even as late as 1816 there were barely 2,000 federal workers with only 500 or so located in Washington, D.C. Early presidents had little in the way of extensive constitutional powers, day-to-day assignments, or a large federal administrative bureaucracy to manage. In fact, George Washington was still able to attend to his farm while he was president.

Besides the relative weakness of the presidency and the small size of the federal bureaucracy, another question that challenged the early national government was the issue of "representation."[6] Disputes over how the federal government and its personnel should represent America were a driving concern of early American public administration.[7] Ensuring that the membership of the federal bureaucracy fairly represented the important interests of the nation was crucial in the early selection of appointments.[8] Those important interests were mainly geographic, with Washington seeking to select men from the diverse states in the Union to ensure that all sections of the new country were represented in his government.

Efforts to ensure that the federal bureaucracy evenly represented different state and local interests were clearly a reaction to King George III's appointment of colonial governors that ignored direct colonial representation. Additionally, the colonists also lacked direct representation in Parliament, although many in England claimed that the colonies' interests were "virtually" represented in Parliament and through the King's administrative appointments in America.[9]

In many ways, the American Revolution was fought largely to protest the Crown's attack on the independence of the local judiciary and the use of royal patronage to reward office seekers at colonial expense. For the signers of the Declaration of Independence, almost all of their complaints involved the abuse of administrative powers by the King.[10] Among the complaints issued against King George III in the Declaration of Independence was that he had "erected a multitude of new offices, and sent hither swarms of officers to harass our people and eat out their substance."[11]

Given such complaints, it is hardly surprising that the first American government, in 1776, emphasized representation rather than administrative efficiency or power. Even though the prime task of the first Continental Congress, building an army and waging war, called for a strong executive, the legislature refused to appoint a chief administrator or even develop departments to serve as adjuncts of Congress. All administration was undertaken by congressional committees, with predictable results.

> John Adams...found himself working eighteen-hour days just to
> keep up with the business of the ninety committees on which he
> served. In one typical case, Congress formed a three member
> committee "to prepare a plan for intercepting two [enemy
> supply] vessels" that were en route to America...This form of
> decision-making doubtless comforted British sea captains, but it
> exasperated almost everyone else.[12]

Not until 1781 did the Continental Congress establish
administrative departments headed by single executives serving at the
pleasure of the legislature.[13] This form of government continued
through the Articles of Confederation. The Articles did not create a
strong central government or even a single office of the presidency.
Power was decentralized, left mainly to the states, and the presidency
was no more than a rotating and powerless office for those serving in
the national legislature. Accordingly, administrative power was "as
fragmented as the general political power from which it stemmed."[14]
The Founding Fathers' ambivalence toward creating a strong national
administrative government was also reflected in the Constitution's
virtual silence on the subject of creating a federal bureaucracy.[15]

Similarly state governments prior to 1776 and at least through
the early nineteenth century had weak executive and administrative
structures. The executive departments in the original thirteen states
were quite weak and as late as the start of the twentieth century most
governors still had short terms and mainly symbolic duties. The
legislature was where the action was, with few states spelling out or
providing for any extensive administrative power or organization.[16]
In part the absence of strong administrative or executive power can
be attributed to a fear of strong central authority, but also because
state governments had few real responsibilities or functions to
perform in 1787 and, thus, there was no need to have much of a state
bureaucracy.

Washington and Adams

Washington pretty much had a free hand in developing the
first federal administration and in determining how public servants

would be selected. Because Washington was the first president and his the first administration, there was neither law nor tradition to dictate how he had to recruit members of his administration or how he had to organize his government. In his appointments, Washington insisted on no overt criteria except "fitness of character." This fitness was measured by "family background, educational attainment, honor and esteem, and, of course, loyalty to the new government—all tempered by a sagacious regard for geographic representation."[17]

The final criterion, geographic diversity, could be regarded as the sole attempt at social representation in an era of "Government by Gentlemen," a government composed of wealthy, well-educated, professional white men and gentry who viewed themselves as the guardians of the American republic. These individuals clearly represented well the demographics of the upper class, as well as those who were entitled to vote because of the property qualifications in place for franchise during this era, not the demographics of the population as a whole. Under Washington and the presidents immediately after, public service was depicted as an honorable and stable occupation for the well-bred and well-educated. Government employees were from the elite, but also considered capable and honest. Removals from office were rare, and nearly always related to performance at work.

Washington's administration, despite its elitist tendencies, also emphasized many values that would guide future administrations. For example, the first administration was bureaucratic in its hierarchic design (the creation of lines of authority from superiors to subordinates), respected establishment of a merit system (honesty, efficiency), and insisted on standard procedures, good record keeping, and use of quantitative data for producing reports and studies. Thus, many of the characteristics that would later be found in legislatively created civil service systems were already found in Washington's administration.

In many ways, the American public service at this time was far more capable and efficient than its far older British counterpart because it was largely free to staff on the basis of competence rather than peerage or tenure.[18] Washington did not use blatant partisanship in choosing his appointees, in part because parties were not yet well developed. Still, he wrote in 1795 that he would not "bring men into any office of consequence knowingly whose political tenets are adverse to the measures the general government is pursuing; for this, in my opinion, would be a sort of political suicide."[19] This ideology gave the public service a pronounced Federalist cast, which was to be reinforced by the more partisan Adams.

One controversy that surfaced during Washington's tenure revolved around presidential removal power. The Constitution was silent on the method for removal of executive officers and employees. In 1789, in House of Representative debates in the first Congress, some, such as William L. Smith of South Carolina, argued that the president had no discretionary power to removal inferior officers and that the only recourse was impeachment.[20] On the other side of the issue was James Madison who was a representative from Virginia and also present during the Constitutional Convention. His position was that the president alone and not Congress had the responsibility and authority to remove federal employees in the executive branch. Madison's arguments prevailed, but the general conflict over the scope of presidential removal power versus congressional control would remain a point of contention even until today.

President Adams continued Washington's appointment strategy. Because of his own personal commitment to integrity and honesty, Adams also valued these characteristics in his appointees. However, society and politics were changing. Under Washington there was minimal political factionalization and no real political parties or party conflict. But, as Washington warned in his farewell address in 1787, parties were beginning to emerge and their appearance should be seen as a dangerous sign of a new source of conflict that could divide America and the government.

Adams's election did see the emergence of rival political parties, with Adams's Federalists and the Jeffersonian Democrats competing against one another. The result was that Adams's appointment strategy was somewhat more political than Washington's.[21]

Adams's administration was transitional in that partisanship started to become important in the appointment process. Perhaps the best example of this partisanship could be found not in appointments to the executive department but in the judiciary which Adams, after losing the presidential election to Jefferson in 1800, sought to pack with last-minute ("midnight") Federalist appointments. Of all the last minute appointments, William Marbury is the most important. Jefferson's refusal to deliver Marbury's judgeship commission after he became president became the basis of the legal conflict that would eventually lead to Chief Justice Marshall's decision in *Marbury v. Madison* that clarified the federal judiciary's power to declare laws of Congress unconstitutional. This decision became the basis of what has become known as judicial review.

Jefferson and the Jeffersonians

Thomas Jefferson's election in 1800 was significant for the federal government in several respects. First, it involved not only a change in party by the president, but both houses of Congress also shifted from Federalist to Democratic-Republican control. All this occurred relatively peacefully, and without the conflict that often marks similar transitions in other new governments. Second, Jefferson's election brought with it increased emphasis on partisanship that would influence federal appointment and service.

By Jefferson's inauguration, the federal government was manned almost entirely by Federalists. The third president responded in contradictory fashion. On the one hand, in 1801 Jefferson stated that partisan activity would not be the basis for removal from office, thus establishing the principle that good behavior and competence were the criteria for officeholding.[22] Yet on the other hand he stated the doctrine that there should be something like "an equal division of offices between the parties." The Federalists hoped this would provoke a public outcry, but then, as now, there was little sympathy for government employees out of work. This was particularly so since the "quality" of the new appointees was not noticeably lower than those they replaced. They were still well educated, upper class, and on the whole honest and capable. For two years Jefferson proceeded to remove Federalists and replace them with Republicans until an approximately equal division of federal positions had been achieved. Afterwards, Jefferson continued to favor Republicans in appointment, but seldom removed incumbent Federalists.[23] In general, Jefferson and his immediate successors "inherited this [Washington's and Adams's appointment] system, had sense enough to leave most of it alone, and saw that it continued to function almost as well as under the Federalists."[24]

The partial and deliberate manner of Jefferson's removals and appointments[25] confirmed his sincerity in proposing an equal division of government offices. Further, his appointment strategy could be defended in terms of modern public administration ideology. Having an approximately equal division of partisans in government makes bureaucracy politically representative of society.[26] Further, a representative distribution of partisans within the bureaucracy enhances the ability of political leadership to change government policy after an executive transition, although competence and efficiency may be sacrificed.

From Government by Gentlemen to the Spoils System

Presidents immediately following Jefferson made somewhat less use of partisanship in appointments, and removals on account of party were quite rare. In part this was true because during the "Era of Good Feeling," presidential-congressional conflict over the federal service was negligible, and party politics again almost disappeared with the continuous triumphs of the Democrats for over 25 years. James Madison did make some use of patronage to maintain support for the War of 1812, but in general the three presidents (James Madison, James Monroe, and John Quincy Adams) "found it difficult to conceive of a public service built on foundations of other than relative tenure, honesty, and reasonable competence."[27]

James Monroe and John Quincy Adams made little use of the congressionally initiated 1820 Tenure of Office Act. This Act made it easier for a clean sweep of the federal bureaucracy in that it limited the terms of many appointed positions to four years. John Quincy Adams thought the law "more congenial to [Democratic-] Republicans out of than to those in office," and for his part even retained men actively opposed to his reelection.[28] This was particularly noteworthy since Adams was the first Federalist elected in twenty-eight years and was relatively unpopular. He needed to build support, and close advisers urged him to do so with partisan appointments. Yet "an unbending integrity and conscience did not permit this President to adopt the political maneuvers of a spoils politician."[29] It was with Andrew Jackson that the partisan and political use of the bureaucracy started to change, and with that change, a new set of political values influenced the organization of the federal government.

Notes

1. Mosher 1982.

2. Kaufman 1956: pp. 1057-1073.

3. Skrowronek 1982.

4. However, even the president's power in foreign affairs was supposed to be limited and exercised concurrently with the Senate. Levy 1988: pp. 30-54.

5. Madison 1937: *Federalist #* 45 and *#* 46.

6. Pitkin 1967: discusses the different meanings surrounding the term "representation."

7. Kaufman 1956.

8. The issue of how the federal bureaucracy should represent America or diverse regional, class, economic, political, or partisan interests remains a question even in recent years with the Reagan presidency clash between career civil servants and political appointees an example of this conflict.

9. Bailyn 1977: pp. 161-175, discusses the disputes over the issue of representation between the colonists and the British.

10. Wilson 1976: p. 101.

11. M. Nelson 1982: p. 750.

12. M. Nelson 1982: pp. 750-751.

13. M. Nelson 1982: p. 751.

14. Van Riper 1958: p. 1.

15. Wilson: 1976, pp. 77-78.

16. Kaufman 1956: p. 1058.

17. Mosher 1968: p. 57.

18. Van Riper, 1958, pp. 18-19; Van Riper 1983, p. 779; M. Nelson, 1982, p. 479.

19. Hoogenboom 1961: p. 4

20. Rakove 1996: p. 170.

21. Rosenbloom 1971: p. 36.

22. Rosenbloom 1971: p. 38.

23. Van Riper: 1958, pp. 18-23.

24. Van Riper, 1983: p. 480.

25. Reaction to Marbury and other "midnight appointments," many of questionable quality, is a notable exception.

26. Krislov & Rosenbloom 1981: pp. 147-148. Goodsell suggests that today's Federal civil service is in fact fairly representative of society, both socially and politically. Obviously this is not true of modern political appointees, who are added and removed with each new administration. Goodsell 1985: pp. 82-86.

27. Van Riper 1958: p. 25.

28. Hoogenboom 1961: p. 5.

29. Van Riper 1958: p. 26.

Chapter III

The Spoils System
from Jackson to Lincoln

Introduction:
Unrepresentative Bureaucracy

The composition of those who served in the federal bureaucracy in the early nineteenth century could hardly be considered
representative of the general population of the United States. The
"government by gentlemen" that existed under the first six presidents
produced a federal service more representative of their landed gentry
background than of the general population. Yet this federal service
was not simply the product of the choice of the first six presidents,
but also of the politics of presidential-congressional interaction
during that time.

Because many of the presidential appointments to the federal
bureaucracy required Senate approval, Congress was able to place
limits upon the president's ability to appoint members to the
executive or judicial branches. Under the first six presidents,
Congress clearly dominated the presidency and therefore the
appointment process and the federal bureaucracy for several reasons.
First, legislative supremacy reflected the philosophy of the Jeffersonians who controlled the national government for most of the period
from 1801–1829. By that, Congress was viewed as the dominant
political force in government and as having more authority than the
president over the federal government. Second, because congressmen
outnumbered civil servants in Washington until the 1820s, the
legislative branch had more personnel and resources to act than did
the federal bureaucracy.[1] Hence, by its very size, Congress was

simply larger than the executive branch.

Third, in the early nineteenth century, Congress de facto selected who would run for president because even though political parties had emerged, political conventions as a means to nominate candidates had yet to arrive.[2] Hence, the major presidential candidates were generally members of Congress. This self-selection process naturally gave Congress significant control over the presidency and perhaps "started a vicious cycle in presidential politics that sometimes made department heads as responsive to Congress, who could advance their own presidential ambitions, as to the president who could not."[3]

Thus, the federal bureaucracy was effectively controlled not by the president alone, but by both the president and Congress. A system of dual control of administration often became one of limited control. Agencies began to "play one branch off against the other; if neither president nor Congress was supreme, then law was, and the agencies interpreted and implemented the law."[4] The federal bureaucracy became somewhat independent from the president and more representative of its own interests.

The ability of public servants to play off one branch against the other both reinforced and was reinforced by their long tenure. While congressional turnover was quite high during the early nineteenth century, public servants in Washington, D.C. tended to grow old in office and often were succeeded by their sons.[5] Even though the 1820 Tenure Office Act sought to limit tenure in office to four years, its impact did little to oust workers from the federal service. Continuity, then as now, gave administrators the knowledge and experience to do their jobs well, but also the power and influence over other Washington actors to maintain their positions. While no legal protections gave federal employees life tenure, they effectively had it and used it to their advantage.[6] In effect, many federal workers came to view their office as a property right and at least one court recognized such a right on the state level.[7]

Because the relationship between Congress and the presidency was so close, it produced a federal service that was demographically unrepresentative. Early presidential administrations, despite early attempts by George Washington to respect geographic representation of sectional interests, were also socially unrepresentative, and could have marked the beginning of a permanent American administrative class countering the nation's emerging focus on (limited) social as well as geographic representation.

However, early American presidents were not representative of the general population. Except for President Fillmore and (arguably) President Garfield, no eighteenth or nineteenth century president was born into modest circumstances.[8] The federal bureaucracy, like the rest of the American political system at this time, was all white, mostly male, and over-represented those from wealthy and elite backgrounds. This was true in both Federalist and Democratic administrations.[9] Criticism that the federal government, including the bureaucracy, did not adequately represent the western states or the common man was the basis of Andrew Jackson's campaign for the presidency, and the Jacksonian creation of the political spoils system.

The Rise of the Spoils System

The election of Andrew Jackson as president in 1828 was a major turning point in American politics.[10] This election gave birth to political parties as significant national forces, and it also marked one of the first elections to see the appearance of national conventions and broadly based franchise premised not on property qualifications. In many ways, Jackson's election redefined the Democratic party in terms of whom it represented and it also initiated a major readjustment of how political parties operated and what relation they would serve vis-a-vis the federal government. By that, Jackson was successful in beginning the process whereby service in federal office was the reward for party work and loyalty, and in making federal employment a source of revenue for the party machinery.[11]

Jackson was perhaps the first outsider elected president. He was not a member of Congress when he became president in 1828. In fact, his election represented a personal triumph over his loss of the presidency in the House of Representatives in 1825 even though he had received the most popular votes in the 1824 election. Hence, Jackson came to office suspicious of Congress and his presidency would be marked by numerous conflicts with the legislative branch.[12]

Jackson was also the first "westerner" elected to the presidency, and he also brought with him representation of a constituency of businessmen and entrepreneurs that contrasted sharply with the land gentry or property owners whose interests characterized and dominated the first six presidents.[13] Because Jackson's election constituted the triumph of a new constituency of voters, it was not surprising that there were demands from these supporters for federal jobs. Hence, demands to replace the existing personnel of the bureaucracy and reward Jackson's supporters fueled the demand for a new vision of how to organize and staff the federal service, i.e., based on personal loyalty and not competence.

Several reasons can account for Jackson's initiation of the spoils system for his supporters. Spoils, in practice although not in name, had already been in place for gentlemen on the national level and it had already been widely implemented on the state and local level through the West and Northeast, though not in the South, which continued in the Federalist tradition of government by gentlemen until the Civil War and in some places long after that.[14] Jackson's use of spoils, hence, was an effort to remove the old class groups in the bureaucracy and put in place his supporters. For Jackson, the impetus for spoils was in part a reform to make the bureaucracy more diverse and representative; at least representative of his supporters.

Extended suffrage, elimination of property qualifications for voting, and the increased costs and resources needed to run a campaign also necessitated that a winner's campaigners and loyal supporters be recruited and rewarded by the spoils of local or federal jobs.[15] Parties, in search of some means to recruit and retain workers, turned to the spoils system as a way to finance their coffers, maintain discipline among the rank and file, and help voters identify whom they should support.[16] For example, in the 1850s the New York customs house was a prime source for patronage. In return for offering loyal supporters jobs at the customs house, weighers, measurers, and gaugers were each required to pay an annual assessment of $25 to the party; inspectors were assessed $15; clerks $15; and night watchmen $7.50. The grand total was over $6,000 in annual assessments paid to the party as a result of receiving a federal job.[17] Hence, the party could use the lure of federal or state employment as a way to buy support and enforce party discipline, place supporters in office and assess them dues, and then use those dues as revenue for campaign and election purposes. The federal service, hence, became no more than a tool of the political parties.

Upon inauguration, Jackson denounced the patronage of old as standing in the way of the mandate that his election had given him.[18] Jackson quickly ordered an examination of administrative expenses to eliminate costs, and within eighteen months 10 percent of the ten-thousand-odd federal employees were replaced, with the president himself removing numerous incumbents and replacing them and others with his supporters.

Despite the eventual use that spoils would have in party building and maintenance, Jackson was only secondarily interested in building his party. His first interests were rewarding supporters and reforming the government. Jackson wished not only to make the public service more democratic (and Democratic), but also to reduce its size.[19] Such economy is hardly conducive to party building by spoils. Unlike most other spoilsmen, Jackson held an idealistic philosophy of administration. For example, Jackson stated in reference to corruption in public office that:

> There are, perhaps, few men who can for any length of time enjoy office and power without being more or less under the influence of feelings unfavorable to the faithful discharge of their public duties...Office is considered as a species of property, and government rather as a means of promoting individual interests than as an instrument created solely for the service of the people. Corruption in some and in others a perversion of correct feelings and principles divert government from its legitimate ends and make it an engine for support of the few at the expense of the many.

Jackson also stated:

> The duties of all public officers are, or at least admit of being made, so plain and simple that men of intelligence may readily qualify themselves for their performance; and I can not but believe that more is lost by the long continuance of men in office than is generally to be gained by their experience.

Finally, the president indicated that public servants have no right to their jobs. Rotation of officials through election can energize and democratize the system.

> ...In a country where offices are created solely for the benefit of the people no one man has any more intrinsic right to official station than another. Offices were not established to give support to particular men at the public expense. No individual wrong is, therefore, done by removal, since neither appointment to nor continuance in office is a matter of right. The incumbent became an officer with a view to public benefits, and when these require his removal they are not to be sacrificed to private interests. It is the people, and they alone, who have the right to complain when a bad officer is substituted for a good one. He who is removed has the same means for obtaining a living that are enjoyed by the millions who never held office. The proposed limitation would destroy the idea of property now so generally connected with official station, and although individual distress may be sometimes produced, it would, by promoting that rotation which constitutes a leading principle in the republican creed, give healthy action to the system.[20]

These comments summarize Jackson's philosophy of reform by spoils, using it as a means of breaking down the power of an entrenched bureaucracy so that it would be more responsive to the president and the people.[21] Yet while Jackson was ideologically motivated, he was not capricious in his removal of federal servants. "The people expect reform—they shall not be disappointed" he wrote Martin Van Buren, but "it must be Judiciously done, and upon principle."[22]

Acting on this reform principle, and spoils was still viewed as a reform in 1828, Jackson slowly and gradually removed incumbent officials and genuinely tried to select able and honest men. Yet it was far from a clean sweep of the bureaucracy. Low level workers were seldom removed. Administratively-experienced chief clerks and employees with needed technical expertise (e.g., in assay offices and the Patent Office) were retained, and the overall percentage of officials dismissed (under twenty percent) was comparable to that of Jefferson's Administration.[23]

Yet one real difference between the organization of the bureaucracy under the Jeffersonians and under the Jacksonians was the long period of political stability which preceded Jackson and had built up government employee expectations of permanence. Under Jackson, that same expectation did not exist and the primary qualification for employment under the government of gentlemen, fitness of character, was amended under the government of the common man to include partisan loyalty and support.

A more important difference between the Jeffersonians and the Jacksonians was Jackson's ideological defense of his practices, and his emphasis on a new social representation. The coalition that had supported and elected Jackson was different from the one which had supported the previous presidents. While previous presidents had been recruited from the east, the original thirteen states, and from landed gentry and aristocracy, Jackson was the first president from the then west (Tennessee), and while it appeared that he represented the democratic frontier and the common man, his support and roots were mainly in the rising commercial and entrepreneurial classes that were fighting against the vested rights and political monopolies of the eastern establishment. The Jacksonian movement was a populism, but a populism of the rising middle class.[24] Jackson "transferred governmental power from one group (the gentry) to another (the politicians)."[25] Transfer of power did not result in a significant change from the elitist structure of the federal bureaucracy, as a comparison of the family backgrounds of the appointments of Adams (Federalist), Jefferson (Democratic), and Jackson reveals.

As Table I suggests, even under Jackson the majority of the appointees came from elite backgrounds, though Jackson did give a greater percentage than before to the middle class. Under none of these presidents was the common man, the farmer, really represented. This questions how much Jackson's election was really a victory for the common man versus the status quo or rising middle class.[26]

Table I
Primary Occupations of Fathers of Presidential
Appointees under Three Presidents[27]

	Adams N=100 %	Jefferson N=104 %	Jackson N=129 %
HIGH-RANKING OCCUPATIONS			
landed gentry	22	29	21
merchant	22	13	17
professional	26	19	15
Total	70	60	53
MIDDLE-RANK OCCUPATIONS	23	25	39
UNKNOWN	7	15	8
Grand Total	100	100	100

The Impact of Jackson's Reforms

Jackson's reforms were popular, but not without controversy. Contrary to what Jackson had believed, some government tasks were not so simple that anyone could do them, such that one could use spoils to replace one person with another. If the mail was not delivered, new lands were not distributed, canals and other public facilities not maintained, the Democrats might well suffer at the polls. The Jacksonian response was to reorganize the government to make public office less complicated and qualifications more uniform: "labor was to be divided, tasks defined, jobs simplified" so that individuals could be placed or replaced (as after an election) without upsetting the system. Spoils bred bureaucracy and a perfection of a division of labor.[28]

Second, though Jackson was principled, the same could not be said of all his supporters. While spoils originated as a reform, it quickly degenerated into simply a tool for party and occasionally personal gain and not as a means to ensure the best qualified for the job. By that, Jackson's politicians were more disposed to steal than their gentry predecessors. For example, his New York City Customs' collector, Samuel Swartout, sailed off to Europe with $1.25 million, a sum equal to five percent of the federal budget! Though Swartout was a standout, lower level embezzling, bribery, and simple malingering were common. However, "the actual proportion of swindlers probably was not much higher than it had been before spoils, despite the conspicuousness of the exceptions. For very sound electoral reasons, 'neither party welcomed scoundrels or irresponsibles in public office...'"[29]

Part of any increase in corruption reflected government growth. The size of the federal government was increasing because its functions were expanding with the size of the country. Large scale land distribution and purchasing authority meant increased opportunity for corruption. On the local level, later nineteenth and early twentieth century Tammany Hall boss George Washington Plunkitt expressed this point by noting that "the old-timers had nothin' to steal, while the politicians now are surrounded by all kinds of temptations..."[30]

The Jacksonian response to corruption was to define duties narrowly to limit the opportunity for fraud. Postmaster General Amos Kendall and others created new audit and accounting units to monitor other parts of government organizations. Yet agencies organized to avoid evil became less efficient and correspondingly less able to do good. Once again, spoils bred bureaucracy as the demand for checks and balances encouraged the hiring of more people to watch over others.[31]

The Jacksonians were notably more disturbed by some types of corruption than others, often ignoring their own corruption. Customs agents made life difficult for merchants who did not support the party in power, finding additional levies or holding cargoes for inspection a long time. Similarly, land offices in the west and Florida helped build the Democratic party by giving the most favorable land grants to Jackson's partisans, and postal officials were known to lose anti-Jackson publications while delivering party journals free of charge.[32] The costs of such corruption were too small to damage party electoral prospects. Indeed, usually the only clear losers were those already in opposition, and the practices actually swelled party coffers and motivated supporters. Not surprisingly, Jackson's successors of both parties long continued such devices.

Jackson's actions and motives were viciously attacked in Congress by his former vice-president, John Calhoun, and by Whig leaders Henry Clay and Daniel Webster. The corruption of spoils gave critics much to attack. Yet their own motives were suspect. Clay had only a few years before urged John Quincy Adams to use appointments for partisan gain. Most proposals involved switching appointment authority from the president to Congress, a move designed more to attack the popular Jackson and enhance the power of the rival Whig party than to present a coherent alternative vision of public administration. If true reform was the goal and this was the best such minds could do, their ability has been greatly overrated.[33]

Perhaps the vehemence of some of the attacks reflected the resentment of a displaced social elite. In the first decades of the nineteenth century, changing social and economic demographics, as well as a changing moral climate, increasingly accorded status to anyone who earned enough money, regardless of social background. Similarly, after suffrage expansion, political power flowed to those best able to secure votes, regardless of morality or social position. At least some of the attacks on Jackson, particularly on his private life, came from former aristocrats who resented government by the common man and instead favored authority by moral or social betters. Many of these men were anti-liberal, favoring moral regulation to promote values and economic regulation to maintain (their) economic positions.[34]

Spoils from Jackson to Lincoln

Had the Jacksonians won thirty years of elections like their Jeffersonian predecessors, it is quite possible that the public service would have entered an era of tranquility like the 1801-29 period. Instead, the Panic of 1837 cut short the presidential career of Martin Van Buren and initiated a period of party instability lasting until the Civil War. Such an instability increased party competition and competition for voters and supporters. This made it even more important to employ spoils as a way to encourage support and produce the revenue needed to support the parties.

Once the Whigs won power in 1840, they quickly forgot their leaders' eloquent attacks on spoils. Officeseekers descended on Washington, and many were satisfied. The process repeated itself four years later when the Democrats returned to the White House. By the time Whig Zachary Taylor took office in 1849, approximately thirty percent of civilian offices were redistributed in the first year of the administration. In 1857, James Buchanan followed spoils to its logical conclusion by replacing the now expected number of appointed officials even though he was succeeding fellow Democrat Franklin Pierce.[35]

The time period was not without worthy innovation. A great many political appointees cared deeply about the efficiency of their organizations. Some based their own appointment and promotion decisions on written examinations or less formal evaluations of efficiency. Concerned by government inefficiency, in 1853 Congress passed legislation that required the examination of some clerks hired in Washington, D.C.[36] This legislation required that most government clerks pass a basic literacy test, the first use of "pass" examinations required by statute. In that year Congress also passed an executive-inspired act long sought by government employees which for the first time established regular pay grades and classifications related to work expectations.

The Beginning of the End for Spoils: Lincoln and the Civil War

Ironically, the most widespread use of spoils in history was made by Lincoln, a president whose core support came from abolitionist moralists who took a dim view of spoils. Of the 1,639 presidential offices that Lincoln could have filled, he replaced personnel in 1,457 of them.[37] During his administration some offices changed personnel two or three times between 1861 and 1865, offering even greater opportunity for Lincoln and the Republican party to reward supporters.[38]

Lincoln used spoils to maintain support for the Civil War, promoting one commentator to contend that "If Lincoln had made appointments for merit only, the war might have been shortened; on the other hand, he might not have preserved a united North to carry on the war."[39] Satirist Artemus Ward quipped that the Union's retreat at Bull Run was caused by a rumor of three vacancies at the New York Customhouse.[40] Further, "had federal agencies been staffed by tenure protected employees before succession, the government might have had to prosecute the war half-full of southern sympathizers, a house divided in the most literal sense."[41]

Conclusion

The spoils system initially developed under Jackson as a reform tactic to replace what was criticized as an elitist bureaucracy with personnel which was more democratic and representative of the interests of the common man. But under Jackson and subsequent presidents, and most particularly under Lincoln, the spoils system became less a reform tactic to make the bureaucracy more accountable and instead it became a patronage tool that presidents and political parties used to reward supporters, recruit new members, and gain control over the personnel of the executive branch. In effect, it tied the structure of the federal government to the changing fortunes and checks imposed by party politics.

While the spoils system received some criticisms from Congress, especially since it was full of Jackson's opponents, it appears to have been relatively efficient though certainly biased in delivering government services. While there was generally little criticism of the spoils system through the Civil War, each president from Jackson to Lincoln used the patronage system to his own advantage.

Notes

1. M. Nelson 1982: pp. 754-756.

2. Pessen 1978: p. 158.

3. M. Nelson 1982: pp. 753-754.

4. M. Nelson 1982: p. 755.

5. M. Nelson 1982: pp. 757-759.

6. More recently, Hugh Heclo has suggested a Gresham's Law in moving civil servants since "it is relatively easy for political executives to get rid of an ethical official...and almost impossible to move a deficient bureaucrat who allies himself with outside political forces and uses the technicalities of the rank-in-job personnel system." Heclo 1977: p. 141.

7. *Hoke v. Henderson*, 15 N.C. 1 (1833).

8. Pessen 1984: pp. 7-34.

9. Mosher 1982: p. 63.

10. Burnham 1970.

11. Pessen 1984: p. 315.

12. Pessen 1984: p. 163.

13. Hofstadter 1989: pp. 64-68; Sellers 1991: p. 299.

14. Van Riper 1958: p. 42.

15. Knott and Miller 1987: p. 17.

16. Kaufman 1956: p. 1059.

17. Rosenbloom 1971: p. 63.

18. Sellers 1991: p. 302.

19. Van Riper 1958: p. 31.

20. All of the above quotes from Van Riper 1958: pp. 36-37.

21. Similar claims are found in Friedman 1983; Peters 1978.

22. Van Riper 1958: p. 35.

23. Hoogenboom 1961: pp. 3-6; Mosher, 1982: p. 62; Van Riper 1958: pp. 49-50.

24. Hofstadter 1973: pp. 72-73.

25. Mosher 1982: p. 63.

26. Aronson 1964: p. 158.

27. Table adapted from Mosher 1982: p. 63.

28. M. Nelson 1982: pp. 760-761.

29. M. Nelson 1982: p. 765.

30. Riordon 1963: p. 32.

31. M. Nelson 1982: pp. 761-763.

32. W. Nelson 1982: pp. 25-27.

33. Van Riper 1958: pp. 37-40; Hoogenboom 1961: pp. 7-8.

34. W. Nelson 1982: pp. 9-12.

35. Van Riper 1958: pp. 41-42.

36. Ingraham 1995: p. 23.

37. Van Riper 1958: p. 43.

38. Hoogenboom 1961: p. 6.

39. Van Riper 1958: p. 43.

40. Van Riper 1958: p. 60.

41. M. Nelson 1982: p. 765.

Chapter IV

The Demise of the Spoils System and the Pendleton Act

Introduction

Passage of the Pendleton Act in 1883 represented a significant change in public administration ethics and organization in the United States. With its adoption, the Pendleton Act signaled both the demise of the spoils system that had started under President Jackson as well as the beginning of a reform movement that would continue through the end of the nineteenth and into the twentieth century. This reform movement sought to remove politics and partisanship from public administration, instituting merit and qualification as the basis for personnel decisions.

Passage of the Pendleton Act, though, required the mobilization of numerous political forces, including public opinion, the media, social reformers, and a heightened conflict between Congress and the president.

The Political Climate of Civil Service Reform

Prior to the end of the Civil War there was sporadic criticism of the spoils system, and patronage hiring enjoyed widespread support as a democratic reform measure.[1] While there were complaints, they were dismissed as grumblings of those out of power. The perceived whiny character of many moralist reformers caused politicos to snicker at "snivel service reform" as effeminate.[2] Spoils politicians often attacked the masculinity of reformers. Senator Ingalls of Kansas, furious at their lack of party unity, once denounced reformers as "the third sex...effeminate without being either masculine or feminine; unable either to beget or bear...endowed with the contempt of men and the derision of women, and doomed to sterility, isolation, and extinction."[3]

Still, there were a few efforts at civil service reform prior to the Civil War. In the 1840s, some in Congress recognized the problems with a politicized bureaucracy where personnel were more worried about their political interests than their official duties. In part, this concern stemmed from political rivalry between Congress and the president. As a result, proposals surfaced during the 1840s for competitive exams, in 1853 for reclassifications of positions, and by 1856, for the establishment of a career civil service, at least for those positions more technical in nature.[4] These efforts either died or made only limited progress.

Even during the Civil War, despite the problems Lincoln had coordinating the federal bureaucracy for the war effort, support for the patronage system persisted. To start with, not all of Lincoln's patronage went to politicians. Many spots were reserved for prominent journalists who could hardly be critical of the spoils system from which they benefited. Spoils received a favorable or mixed press until Lincoln's successors failed to court newspaper support in this manner.[5] Similarly, more than a few diplomatic positions were filled with well-educated abolitionists, endearing Lincoln to those intellectuals who would later lead the reform movement against spoils.[6]

Yet Lincoln's sweeping aside of experienced Democratic party officials at a time when federal responsibilities were expanded by the war caused serious administrative problems.[7] By the end of the Civil War there were 53,000 federal workers with a payroll of $30,000,000.[8] With seven major federal departments, there was little in the way of coordination among the different branches of government. There was little distinction between policy making and lower level administrative positions, no uniformity in position qualifications, and many of those holding technical positions were unqualified. Finally, the tenure of most civil servants was quite short, often well under four years,[9] and Lincoln's frequent replacement of personnel to augment the war effort left few bureaucrats with much experience and the bureaucracy as a whole with very little stability. Naturally, these problems hampered the mobilization of the North against the South.

These administrative problems did not escape Lincoln's supporters and opponents. In early 1864 Massachusetts Senator Charles Sumner introduced a bill providing for appointment by competitive examinations with implementation by a civil service commission. Though Sumner had long been interested in government administration, the timing of his bill and his opposition to the president suggested an effort to embarrass a Lincoln machine manned by officeholders. Sumner did not strongly push his bill and it failed, but the proposal did attract some support among academics, reform Republicans, and journalists.

Their backing rematerialized when Rhode Island Congressman Thomas Jenckes, a Lincoln supporter, waited until after the Civil War to introduce his bill to establish a competitive civil service.[10] Despite some backing from intellectuals and many prominent newspapers and magazines including *Harper's Weekly* and the *North American Review*, Jenckes's bill attracted little initial support in Congress. Later on, support for Jenckes' bill reflected hostility to Lincoln's hapless successor, Andrew Johnson, and a desire among many congressman to obtain their fair share of spoils from the bureaucracy.[11]

Yet in 1865 most of the public still saw spoils as proper and reasonably efficient. Bureaucratic reform was often seen more as "something Prussian" than something democratic. As Vermont congressman Frederick Woodbridge pointed out, the merit system was used in aristocratic societies where rail splitters did not become leaders. It "might work in Belgium, France, or England, where the masses are mere machines; but in America it will never work." [12]

The Political Basis of Civil Service Reform

Several long-term forces tended to advance reform of the spoils system. First, certain business interests, among them, the American Manufacturers Association, were dissatisfied with traditional corruption. Growing in numbers and increasingly important, urban merchants[13] were distressed by the costs and delays of a corrupt customs system, and they began to lobby for reform. Their support in part came from claims by Jenckes who appealed to businessmen eager to cut taxes, arguing that a merit service would cut one-third of federal employment and increase by half the efficiency of remaining workers.[14] Efficiency arguments did not attract much notice until the scientific management movement around the turn of the twentieth century.

Yet the efficiency issue partly explains stronger support for Jenckes's bill among urban than among rural congressmen. Under such pressure in 1874, for example, Congress reformed the New York Customhouse and other large ports, decreasing the payroll and eliminating the system under which port inspectors could collect a large portion of confiscated goods. This removed much of the revenue associated with the importation of goods, lessening the parties' stake in the system.[15]

Federal employees were a lesser, though still important interest favoring reform of the spoils system. A poll conducted by Jenckes's committee found that 362 of 374 middle level government administrators responding (out of a sample of 446) favored the reform bill.[16] Federal workers certainly had strong incentive to work for the protection of their jobs, and for administrators, merely holding those jobs under spoils demonstrated some political influence. Also, the presence of intellectuals and former journalists in Lincoln's administration and their absence in previous and later administrations made these rather important groups desirous of change.[17]

Second, foreign experience with bureaucracy encouraged American civil service reformers. While some thought innovations from Britain and Prussia were threatening to democracy, to others foreign experience demonstrated the potential of a merit system based on examinations. In arguing for civil service reform, Jenckes noted the bureaucratic efficiency of the Prussian army in the Austro-Prussian War.[18] Certainly this compared favorably with Union performance in the Civil War in which, reformers argued, the incompetence of Union administration cost the lives of thousands of soldiers.[19] Army reformers were also impressed by the comparison. They sought merit promotion, a general staff insulated from politics, a coherent system of military education, and other reforms well into the twentieth century.[20]

Similarly, Jenckes and others were impressed with the relative efficiency and honesty of mail service in Britain and elsewhere. Reformers saw bureaucracy as a progressive innovation which America needed to be as modern as Europe. Indeed, a report issued by Jenckes in 1868 contains some eighty-two pages detailing Chinese, Prussian, French, and especially English civil service procedures. Among other things, Jenckes and others believed that a merit service could bring needed intellectuals into government.[21] Conversely, participants in the spoils system were not beyond accepting foreign bureaucratic innovation. For example, in 1862 Secretary of State William Seward commissioned a study of the French tax collection bureaucracy to improve American revenue collection.[22] But many critics of reform saw a merit system as un-American and antidemocratic.

Another political force behind the reform movement was rooted in the hostility between President Andrew Johnson, a southerner, and the radical Republican Congress. While part of the conflict over civil service reform was rooted in ideological disagreements over the direction and leadership of the reconstruction of the South after the Civil War, their disagreements over reform had other sources as well. One, because Congress did not trust President Johnson in his Reconstruction efforts, and because the radical Republicans had different views on the status of the African-Americans, Congress sought to reassert itself and assume a leadership role in the federal government that it had lost under Lincoln. Thus, many of the conflicts between the two were really rooted in separation of powers and national leadership questions with Congress doing what it could to control the president by overriding his vetoes, passing a Tenure of Office Act in 1867 that placed limits upon presidential removal power, and by impeaching Johnson and almost having him thrown out of office.

A second source of congressional-presidential conflict over

civil service reform was rooted in the desire of many congressmen to obtain their fair share of spoils that they had missed out on during the rapid growth of the bureaucracy during the Civil War. In many ways, once Johnson became president, early calls for reform were mainly congressional and radical Republican party demands to capture the federal bureaucracy and use the spoils system to their advantage. Demand for the reform of the spoils movement, thus, was in the 1860s rooted in the congressional acceptance of spoils, in a desire to use it to augment legislative power over the president, and in a desire to use spoils to the personal benefit of many congressmen.

The Moral Basis of Civil Service Reform

In addition to political forces propelling changes in administrative organization, the persistent corruption of the spoils system generated demands from religious groups and intellectuals that moral reform of the federal government was required. Early reformers were interested first in morality and "only secondarily — and not a very close second at that...in efficiency and economy, the dollars and cents value of the merit system."[23] The "Wanted-Situations" columns of the *Star* and other Washington newspapers often carried such advertisements as "$100 cash and 10% of salary for one year, will be given for a Position in any of the Departments."[24] It was also common practice among many politicians to issue special yearly assessments to their appointees, forcing them to contribute to their boss's campaign or political party. Spoils created a form of political kickbacks and were a source of scandal that later legislation sought to outlaw.[25]

Reformers were quick to paint the immoral character of political assessments and spoils in sensationalist propaganda. One wailed that after an election:

> Some young women in despair, losing hope at the loss of their jobs, went wrong on the town...Oh! the pity of it...the oldest trade in the world hospitally [sic] extended a welcome to these unfortunate recruits, and the folks back home unknowingly

continued to enjoy the wages of an erring daughter whom of course they still thought a government employee.[26]

In many ways, the moralistic focus on spoils in part represented an attempt to apply antislavery moral precepts to political life. Former abolitionists who had always placed moral values above the majority rule favored by Jacksonians sought to moralize government by placing in it men of Christian character.[27] The spoilsman "replaced the slave owner as the jinni of evil."[28] Further, the public administration of the Founding Fathers and the government by gentlemen offered useful and not wholly incorrect myths about the moral glory of government past.[29] Yet where the Founding Fathers were wanting, reformers could rewrite history to demonstrate their true merit compared to the spoilsmen usurpers. Henry Adams, for example, found Jefferson's removal of Federalists to be a reluctant act forced on him by supporters. Even then Jefferson sought to "injure the best men least."[30] In this old bureaucratic model, reformers thought they had found a modern means for abolishing party politics and bringing morals back in.[31]

One conclusion is that the battle over spoils reflected a clash between two competing political cultures, one moralistic and one individualistic, which still divide American politics.[32] The moralistic world of the abolitionist reformers derived its origins in New England Puritan township beginnings, where politics were the responsibility of each citizen and should be pursued for the good of the whole community. Political issues should reflect not competing material stakes but rather distinct ideological visions of the good society.

Moralists generally employ purposive or ideological incentives to maintain their political organizations.[33] For the reformers in the 1860s, as well as even today, moralists tended to view bureaucracy favorably since it (supposedly) brought desirable political neutrality and enhanced the government's ability to implement good policies. Moral reform of the bureaucracy, in many ways, was tied into a desire for moral regeneration or purification of the American political system and an attempt to root out the corruption of money that spoils and patronage caused.

The individualistic political culture evolved from the marketplace agrarianism of the Middle Atlantic colonies, where politics eschewed ideological concerns and was viewed in narrow utilitarian terms. Political leaders are to give the public what it wants rather than what is right, and people have no obligation to act politically if they can better their positions in other ways.[34] Not surprisingly, personal exchange and obligation were held above civic ideals, and political machines are held together by individual solidary and material incentives.[35]

The individualistic political culture seemingly held by many spoilsmen tended to view bureaucracy as a source of favor, patronage, and reward, and it was less directly concerned with corruption or inefficiency. Were ideological defenses given to the spoils system, they would have claimed that spoils aided democracy, promoted accountability, helped sustain political parties, and encouraged participation and civil duty.[36]

A good example of this individualistic political culture is found in the late nineteenth and early twentieth century Tammany Hall boss George Washington Plunkett's laments on the end of "patriotism" with the rise of civil service:

> [W]hen a party won, its workers got everything in sight. That was something to make a man patriotic. Now, when a party wins and its men come forward and ask for their rewards, the reply is "Nothin' doin'...The boys and men don't get excited any more when they see a United States flag or hear "The Star Spangled Banner." They don't care no more for firecrackers on the Fourth of July. And why should they? What is there in it for them?[37]

Yet as the conflicts over reform in the post-Civil War era demonstrated, difficulties could occur when bosses and reformers worked together.

> Thus Woodrow Wilson in New Jersey and Joseph Folk in Missouri were made, respectively, Governor and Attorney General through agreements with bosses, and both turned on their benefactors, Wilson in matters of program and patronage, Folk to the extent of a prosecution for corruption. To bosses Jim

Smith and Ed Butler, Wilson and Folk were ingrates and scoundrels. But in their own minds the reformers were justified in placing civic ideals and public commitments over and above mere personal obligations.[38]

Of course, spoils was hardly the only source of corruption. Even after the worst aspects of the system were reformed years later, New York City Tammany Hall boss George Washington Plunkitt eloquently described the ease with which one could make a "legal" fortune in politics through real estate manipulations and advance knowledge of public sales and purchases. As Plunkitt again remarked, "The politician who steals is worse than a thief. He is a fool. With the grand opportunities all around for the man with a political pull, there's no excuse for stealin' a cent."[39]

Spoils served as the main target of reformers in this era because it came to symbolize the whole corrupt individualistic culture, and most moralists assumed that the administrative problems would melt away if those in government were morally good and honest.

Finally, as in Jackson's day, class consciousness was one source of support for and opposition to bureaucratic restructuring. Nearly all reform leaders were Yankees, and most were the well educated and rather well-to-do sons of established businessmen or professionals. The average reformers were

lawyers, editors, clergymen, professors, and businessmen whose interests were mercantile and financial rather than industrial. The typical reformer came from an old-established New England family...(and he) was either an Episcopalian or a Unitarian and was a Harvard graduate. Proud of his Anglo-Saxon heritage, he patterned his thoughts and actions after English models. John Stuart Mill was his philosopher and William E. Gladstone his ideal statesman.[40]

Many of these reformers were suspicious of those with lesser background, and who were serving in the bureaucracy, and more than a few were skeptical of universal suffrage. Others such as E. L. Godkin and John Kasson argued that majority rule worked in small towns where nearly all voters owned property and accordingly had an interest in the long term good of the polity. It failed, however, where few owned property. The poor were likely to sell their votes for a few dollars or else settle for short term raids on the rich rather than long term good government.[41] Reformers' attachment to the "right" sort of people is demonstrated by their disdain for spoils politicians who themselves adopted reforms.

For example, in the 1870s, Grant's Treasury Secretary, George Boutwell, ran his department in an exemplary fashion, carefully devising and implementing a merit system based on examinations and performance ratings years before any serious pressure to do so. Yet he was consistently attacked by reformers, perhaps because he was undertaking his duties not out of sense of moral reform but for very individualistic reasons.[42]

Yet along with a class consciousness, a "nativism" bias was a further source of support for civil service reform. Increasingly, Americans distrusted the (mainly Irish) immigrants who could often outvote them in urban elections. The New York draft riots of 1863 and the Tweed Ring hardened Nativist thinking, thus leading to a backlash against the Irish and other nationalities perceived to be inferior.[43]

Presidential Politics and Support for Civil Service Reform

Perhaps the most important long term factors pushing for reform were the interests of politicians and the drama of presidential politics. Spoils could hold a party together, and that was one of the reasons the Jacksonians and subsequent presidents supported it. But spoils could also tear a party apart. As early as Jefferson, politicians realized that each appointment could spawn ten enemies and one ingrate, and the sheer crush of officeseekers who descended on Washington, D.C., after each election could prove unpleasant and time-consuming. Indeed, Democrat Grover Cleveland publicly encouraged the post-election conversions of his lame duck Republican predecessor appointees to civil service, expressing his desire to avoid such distraction.[44]

Generally, except for the Democrat Cleveland, the Republican presidents between Lincoln and Theodore Roosevelt were politically weak and generally ambivalent about civil service reform. In the 1870s and 1880s, civil service reform became more of a presidential than a congressional issue because the cause was a way for presidents to regain control over an appointment power that had eroded to Congress during the Johnson administration. Henry Adams, in an important essay in the *Nation*, stated that the root issue in the reform movement was a loss of power among many constituencies, including the president, and how to use reform as a way to increase it over the federal bureaucracy.[45]

Congress, except for moralistic reformers like Jenckes, strongly opposed reform measures. In part opposition reflected legislators' interest and newly obtained power after the Civil War to influence presidential appointments to reward friends and maintain support. Only when Congress felt it was losing control of the spoils system did it advocate reform.

Fears of rebel subversion were also important and more than a few congressmen were quick to wave the bloody shirt. An Indianan, for example, held up the frightening prospect that a graduate of Virginia's Washington College, of which Robert E. Lee was president, would do better on a civil service examination than a disabled soldier of some "common school or workshop of the West, who lost a limb at the battle of Chickamauga."[46]

As Democratic presidential candidates lost each election from 1860 to 1880, many of the Party of Jackson reconsidered the virtues of unvarnished majority rule and administration, and support civil service reform.[47] In 1876, the Democrats nominated pro-reform Samuel J. Tilden, who as New York Governor put reform into practice by helping the crusade against Boss Tweed. He so successfully moved against corruption and pork in government that state taxes were soon one-third their former level![48] Democrats saw reform and bureaucratization as a means of weakening the Republican hold on federal jobs. Incumbent presidents and congressmen always had good reason to favor tenuring government workers if they lost or expected to lose the next election. Therefore each lame duck president in the era, and indeed, as late as 1953, extended the number of protected positions.

Despite the long term forces driving policy, several events were needed to gain passage of the Pendleton Act and extend the civil service from its minuscule beginnings. As is mentioned above, distrust of President Johnson gave Jenckes's initiative a boost. Though considered basically in favor of reform, and viewed as a reform candidate in 1868, Grant's initial appointments actually offended both spoilsmen and reformers by giving positions to his personal friends rather than those of any significant political camp.[49] Grant, unlike Lincoln, also failed to appoint many journalists to his administration. Soon the press, including the *New York Times*, *Harper's Weekly*, and the *Nation*, were whipping up public opinion and criticizing the president for not supporting the cause of reform. Along with intense press pressure, the GOP defeat in the 1870 midterm elections, coupled with success of reform Republican candidates in Missouri and elsewhere, led Grant to weakly support congressional moves toward reform. In 1871 a joint resolution enabling the President to establish a Civil Service Commission passed a lame duck Congress.[50]

To the surprise of many, Grant responded to congressional and press pressure and adopted many reforms. For example, in 1873 the President issued an executive order banning federal civil servants from holding local offices. More importantly, Grant established a Civil Service Commission, staffed it with some prominent reformers, and at first enacted some of its regulations. By 1872 the Commission classified federal grades, established procedures for competitive examinations, and recommended the end of political assessments. Grant at first adopted these regulations through executive order, but in 1873 allowed the Commission to die for lack of funds. He also appointed many commissioners who were not as committed to reform ashad been thought. Grant later rescinded the rules, most of which had not been widely implemented anyway.[51] Still, the short-lived regulations served as a model for the Pendleton Act and later reforms.

Indeed,

> Much of the terminology and many of the concepts employed in the proceedings, reports, and other recorded activities of the Commission still prevail. Among these are: "Civil Service Commission rules," "application," "test," "grade," "eligible," "ineligible," "register," "military preference," "position," "vacancy," "apportionment," "probation," "promotion," "classification," "superannuation," "political assessments," "pernicious political activity," "boards of examiners," "ratings of 70 per cent," "three highest eligible," "policy-deciding officials," "certificate," and many others.[52]

While Commission activities fleshed out reform proposals, the pervasive corruption of the Grant era helped prepare public opinion. The Whiskey Ring, the Credit Mobilier scandal, and War Secretary Belknap's selling of Indian post traderships also tended to undermine the legitimacy of the spoils system. These scandals might have hurt only the Republican Party, were it not for the Tweed Ring and other state and local Democratic counterparts which also damaged the reputation of spoils. In addition to outright corruption, the salary grab of 1873, in which Congress voted itself a fifty percent pay increase retroactive to December 1871, certainly helped focus political debate on the morality of government.[53]

Of equal importance were the organizing efforts of reformers. Reform Republicans increasingly sought to take over state conventions, with some success. Some even broke away from the Party to support Horace Greeley, whose stand on reform was ambiguous in the 1872 presidential contest. Still, their political effectiveness was limited by internal divisions over free trade and Reconstruction.[54] More importantly, in 1877, well-off attorney Dorman Eaton, the actual author of what would eventually become the Pendleton Bill, and others founded the first Civil Service Reform Association in New York.[55] The organization faltered at first, but by 1880 had many affiliates in other states. In 1881 the National Civil Service Reform League (NCSRL) was founded, and for the next twenty years or so pushed for a variety of civil service reforms.[56]

In 1876 the Republicans nominated Rutherford B. Hayes, the moderately pro-reform Ohio governor who had managed to offend no major factions in the party. Hayes won a close, corrupt election over pro-reform candidate Tilden. Fittingly, he moved incrementally in office, pleasing neither reformers nor spoilsmen. Hayes appointed a mainly pro-reform Cabinet, commissioned Eaton to do a study of the British civil service, and issued an executive order officially enforcing an 1876 law against assessments. In *Ex parte Curtis*,[57] the Supreme Court upheld the ban on assessments, noting that it was well within the power of Congress to pass legislation to promote efficiency, integrity, and proper discipline in public service and that it was permissible for Congress to "prevent those in power from requiring help for such [political] purposes as a condition to continued employment."[58] Unfortunately, serious implementation was spotty.[59]

Yet Hayes did take on notorious New York Republican Party boss Roscoe Conkling, but this was mainly a personal struggle. Conkling had been a relatively honest spoilsman. He did not strongly oppose a merit system, and he placed reasonably efficient underlings in offices he controlled. He was doomed by his opposition to Hayes and the president painted the battle against the Conkling-controlled New York Customhouse as a reform crusade.[60]

In 1880 the GOP nominated Ohio congressman James Garfield, who had led many reform battles in Congress. President Garfield proved as weak as he was short-lived. He opposed assessment, yet made unparalleled use of it in winning a close election. Personally honest, he made no effort to investigate the Star Route frauds through which Hayes's postal officials siphoned off hundreds of thousands for Party and personal use. Similarly, when Ohio Democratic Senator George Pendleton[61] introduced a bill to reestablish the Civil Service Commission and set up a tenured merit system based on competitive examinations, Garfield indicated that "pass" exams were adequate and the Pendleton Bill went too far.[62]

Yet as Garfield single handedly pushed the Pendleton Bill forward, he was assassinated by a "disappointed office seeker." The wrenching manner of Garfield's death (he lingered for over ten weeks) as well as the comparison between the Civil War general of modest birth and his depraved killer, made the president a national hero and forever soiled the image of spoils.[63] Intellectual reformers were quick to rewrite Garfield's brief presidency, making him a lion for reform rather than a spineless tool of the spoilsmen.

Pendleton himself reproached the spoils system with reports of Garfield's delirious cry, "Do tell that crowd of office-seekers I cannot see them today—I am so sick."[64]

The Pendleton Act, basically a Democrat sponsored measure, would still have failed had not the Republicans suffered a serious setback in the 1882 election. Foreseeing defeat in the next presidential election, the GOP found civil service much to its liking and endorsed the Democratic initiative. President Arthur, who had succeeded Garfield, even called for passage of the Pendleton Bill.[65] This chorus of support led the *New York Tribune*, among others, to remarked that "now it is delightful to see the zeal of these new converts preaching the blessed truth that those who are in ought not to be put out."[66] Thus, by 1883, both parties were too closely tied to reform to pull out, assuring the passage of the first major civil service merit system in the United States. The only major debates that would occur in Congress were over how broad the bill would be, and how many and what positions the bill would eventually cover. In the final congressional votes, there were clear breaks in sectional support for civil service reform, with the East strongly pro-reform and the West and South generally against it.

Spoils and Representation

To a considerable degree, the debate over spoils before the Pendleton Act, and to an even greater degree after, concerned the meaning, nature, and role of administration in a democracy. Government administration can be seen as a mere tool to accomplish the goals of government, or as a part of government itself. The former position would render unimportant those who served in government below the elected level because these civil servants would merely be carrying out the will of elected policymakers. This view supported a politics/administration dichotomy where policymaking and administration would be distinguished so that politics would not be an issue in the bureaucracy. Such a dichotomy would suggest that a bureaucracy should be more concerned with competence and fitness for the job, and not how well it represented outside interests except at the highest levels.

No one involved in the civil service debates of the 1870s and 1880s seemed to hold this view. Certainly reformers wanted more intellectual Yankees in service and spoilsmen wanted politicians, yet both agreed that democratic administrative structures should be staffed by a population at least somewhat like the public at large, although there were few demands for the entry of women, Blacks, or Native Americans into the bureaucracy. Beyond these important exceptions, both sides favored "descriptive representation" as it is now known. It is not enough for a democratic government to act in a fashion suggested or affirmed by election. Rather, legitimacy requires that those in government resemble society demographically.[67]

Since the embryonic civil service system set up by the Pendleton Act was based on examinations, and none save a few had much opportunity in government anyway, education was important. Still, the main demographic criterion was geography, as it was during Washington's administration. To satisfy geographic representation, the Pendleton Act included geographic "apportionment" of Washington offices among the states, based on population, and to be followed "as nearly as practicable."[68] Still, there was the fear of educational elitism, reinforced by doubts that examination scores would have any relationship to work ability. As Representative McKee of Mississippi complained:

> Suppose some wild mustang girl from New Mexico comes here for a position, and it may be that she does not know whether the Gulf stream runs north or south, or perhaps she thinks it stands on end, and she may answer that the "Japan current" is closely allied to the English gooseberry, yet although competent for the minor position she seeks, she is sent back home rejected, and the place is given to some spectacled school ma'am who probably has not half as much native sense as the New Mexico girl.[69]

To see that this did not happen, it was specified that examinations be "practical in character" and as closely as possible related to the duties to be performed. This was far different from British examinations, which favored those with a classic education no matter the job, though generally only relatively high level jobs were included in the system. Notably, job-related tests required the first careful analysis of the skills used in a variety of jobs.[70]

Reformers argued that a merit-based civil service need not be undemocratic simply because it was employed by Old World monarchies; a different examination scheme and other measures could see to that. Jenckes argued in the 1860s that a merit system could be truly democratic and fair because under it office could be gained by ordinary citizens who lacked political connections. Pendleton made the same argument fifteen years later, and pointed out that exams employed in the reformed New York Customhouse did not necessarily favor those with college degrees.[71]

The issue of bureaucratic accountability to political control was only touched on in the early reform/spoils debates. Echoing Jackson, Illinois Representative John Logan complained to Jenckes:

> This bill is an opening wedge to an aristocracy in this country...It will lead us to the point where there will be two national schools in this country---one for the military and the other for civil education. These schools will monopolize all avenues of approach to the Government. Unless a man can pass one or another of these schools and be enrolled upon their lists he cannot receive employment under this Government, no matter how great may be his capacity, how indisputable may be his qualifications. When once he does pass this school and fixes himself for life his next care will be to get his children there also. In these schools the scholars will soon come to believe that they are the only persons qualified to administer the Government, and soon come to resolve that the Government will be administered by them and by none others.[72]

Such fears were understandable, given the "Oxbridge" domination and perceived elitism of the British civil service.[73] The practical nature of American exams, geographic quotas, and the Pendleton Act's strictures against nepotism were meant to make such domination unlikely.

Of equal importance also was the open nature of the American service. The British and most other merit systems were open only at the bottom or for entry level positions. In contrast, Pendleton assured an American civil service open to new talent at all levels. This is still the case, and of course makes political infiltration of the career service possible.[74] It has also assured that a permanent civil service or administrative class would not emerge and close the bureaucracy to outsiders.

Conclusion

By 1883, the battle against the spoils system was not over, but the passage of the Pendleton Act, along with other national and state level attempts to root out corruption and reform the bureaucracy, clearly suggested that the support for spoils and government by the common man was on the way out. Political conflicts between Congress and the president over patronage were important pushes for reforms but this new ideology of public administration was a reform movement clearly influenced by moral and religious concerns that patronage, spoils, and the unbridled competition for office were not democratic and supportive of good accountable government. It stood for the opposite. The reform movement took up the language of democracy, appealed to traditional American principles and fears of corruption, and sought to create a civil service that would be more politically neutral, independent, and competent.

Passage of the Pendleton Bill in 1883 was not to be the climax of the civil service reform movement, but simply the start. Only a few entry level positions were covered by the law. For the next seventy years future presidents would reclassify and place more and more positions under some type of competitive examination civil service system until over ninety percent of the federal jobs were classified that way. This left only a few thousand jobs available to spoils.

Notes

1. Hoogenboom 1961: p. 7.

2. Van Riper 1958: pp. 61-62; Hoogenboom 1961: pp. 30-31.

3. Hofstadter 1963: pp. 185-196. Such charges were later partly dispelled by the macho style of reformer Theodore Roosevelt who would endorse civil service reform during the Progressive Era.

4. Hoogenboom 1961: p. 9.

5. Hoogenboom 1961: p. 63.

6. Hofstadter 1963: pp. 172-174.

7. Hoogenboom 1961: p. 9.

8. Hoogenboom 1961: p. 1.

9. Hoogenboom 1961: p. 5.

10. Hoogenboom 1961: pp. 10-11, 15.

11. Hoogenboom 1961: pp. 15, 17, 27-28.

12. Hoogenboom 1961: p. 30.

13. Jenckes appealed to other businessmen eager to cut taxes, arguing that a merit service would cut one-third of federal employment and increase by half the efficiency of remaining workers. Hoogenboom 1961: p. 28. The efficiency argument was not to attract much notice, however, until the scientific management movement.

14. Hoogenboom 1961: p. 28.

15. Skowronek 1961: pp. 31, 103-105, 131-132.

16. Hoogenboom 1961: pp. 44-45.

17. Hofstadter 1964: pp. 172-180.

18. Hoogenboom 1961: p. 31.

19. M. Nelson 1982: p. 765.

20. Skowronek 1982: pp. 88-92, 213-228.

21. Hoogenboom 1961: p. 14; Skowronek 1982: pp. 48-55; Van Riper 1958: p. 64.

22. Van Riper 1958: p. 64.

23. Van Riper 1958: p. 85.

24. M. Nelson 1982: p. 765.

25. Hoogenboom 1961: p. 226.

26. M. Nelson, 1982: p. 765.

27. W. Nelson 1982: pp. 62-67.

28. Van Riper 1958: p. 81.

29. Where the Founding Fathers were wanting, reformers could rewrite history to demonstrate their true merit compared to the spoilsmen usurpers. Henry Adams, for example, found Jefferson's removal of Federalists to be a reluctant act forced on him by supporters. W. Nelson 1982: pp. 88-90. Even then, Jefferson sought to "injure the best men least." W. Nelson 1982: p. 89.

30. W. Nelson 1982: pp. 88-90.

31. W. Nelson 1982: pp. 82-83, 87-88.

32. Elazar 1972.

33. Clark 1961: pp. 129-166.

34. Cook 1996: pp. 4-6 makes a similar point in contrasting competing roles for the bureaucracy as either a source of social education and inculcation of values versus viewing the bureaucracy merely as an instrumental source of delivering goods.

35. Wilson 1973.

36. Far less important for our purposes is the traditionalistic political culture which reflects Southern plantation agriculture. It values the continuation of societal traditions and invests authority in a small, homogeneous social elite, discouraging participation by others. This political culture perhaps confronts a merit system's possible disruption of elite rule based on personal relationships and, thus, would resist reform. Elazar 1972: pp. 93-103.

37. Riordon 1963: p. 15.

38. Hofstadter 1955: p. 23.

39. Riordon 1963: pp. 3-6, 29-32.

40. Hoogenboom 1961: p. 21.

41. Schiesl 1977: pp. 8-9; Hofstadter 1964: pp. 175-178; W. Nelson 1982: pp. 89-90.

42. Hoogenboom 1961: pp. 68-69.

43. Callow 1965: pp. 262-268.

44. Van Riper 1958: p. 132.

45. Hoogenboom 1961: p. 67.

46. Hofstadter 1964: p. 182.

47. W. Nelson 1982: p. 63.

48. Kelley 1979: p. 260; Hoogenboom 1961: p. 142.

49. Hoogenboom 1961: pp. 53-56, 74-75, 78-79.

50. Hoogenboom 1961: pp. 86-88.

51. Hoogenboom 1961: pp. 90-96, 108; Van Riper 1958: p. 71.

52. Van Riper 1958: p. 70.

53. Van Riper 1958: p. 74.

54. Hoogenboom 1961: pp. 112-118.

55. Hoogenboom 1961: pp. 190-193.

56. Hoogenboom 1961: pp. 187-189, 211.

57. 106 U.S. 371 (1882).

58. *Ibid.* 375.

59. Hoogenboom 1961: pp. 140-141; Van Riper 1983: p. 478.

60. Hoogenboom 1961: pp. 155-178.

61. Interestingly, Pendleton had never particularly favored a merit service, and was probably personally corrupt. Yet he also had an enduring interest in the machinery of government. For example, he once proposed giving Cabinet officers seats in Congress. Hoogenboom 1961: pp. 200-201.

62. Hoogenboom 1961: pp. 199-208.

63. Rosenberg 1968.

64. Hoogenboom 1961: p. 217.

65. Hoogenboom 1961: p. 237.

66. Van Riper 1958: p. 94.

67. Pitkin 1972: pp. 80-81.

68. Van Riper 1958: p. 101. This is still the case even today, and can make it relatively difficult for residents of Maryland or Virginia to find positions. Pincus 1978: p. 169.

69. Hofstadter 1964: p. 183.

70. Van Riper 1958: pp. 72-73, 100.

71. Hoogenboom 1961: pp. 30-31, 238; Hofstadter 1963: p. 185.

72. Hofstadter 1964: pp. 181-182.

73. Plowden 1984: pp. 29-30.

74. Van Riper 1958: p. 101.

Chapter V

The Politics/Administration Dichotomy During the Progressive Era

Introduction: The Transformation of Civil Service Reform

The civil service reform movement underwent several important changes after passage of the Pendleton Act in 1883. First, passage of the Act was not a complete remedy for all the social and political ills facing the federal government. Other problems persisted, such as mismanagement and local corruption, but the Pendleton Act could not address them. In part this was because the Act covered only a very small percentage of the positions in the federal government, such as entry level and clerical positions in urban centers and where custom houses were located. Also, the reform spirit somewhat lapsed on the federal level after 1883 and some hostility against the Act developed in Congress, leading to unsuccessful efforts to repeal it.

Most of the reform effort after 1883 shifted to state and municipal corruption where passage of local versions of the Pendleton Act was sought. But even on the state and local level, reform efforts soon lost appeal as reform candidates, including Pendleton, lost elections. The fear of corruption, so intense only a few years ago, had lost much of its steam as a political rallying point.

Even on the presidential level there were some questions regarding the viability of reform. During the 1880s and 1890s reform was a minor issue eclipsed by the demands of farmers to solve numerous agriculture and free currency problems. Unlike a decade earlier, William Jennings Bryan and the Democrats opposed the merit system in the 1896 election. The spirit of the Populist movement opposed the merit system much in the same way that the Jacksonians opposed the government by gentlemen as elitist and anti-democratic.[1]

While the reform movement did change and lose some of its momentum after 1883, it was not dead. The movement changed in at least three important ways. First, starting in the late 1890s and into the early twentieth century, there was a new focus to reform. Partly as a result of the Populist movement, reformers became preoccupied with efforts to reconcile the operation of the federal bureaucracy with the basic political values of representative democracy. Reformers asked how a politically-neutral merit system and a tenured civil service could operate within a political system that respected representative democracy and public accountability of public office holders through competitive elections. One solution to this problem would be to try to distinguish politics from administration and push the goal of neutral competence.

A second problem that would preoccupy reformers developed in the early twentieth century Progressive Era. While early reformers stressed rooting out moral corruption as the impetus for reform, the Progressives became increasingly more concerned with efficiency and economy as a goal of bureaucratic reform. During the early twentieth century, the federal government sought to professionalize the civil service, adopting many business practices to improve the efficiency and organization of the bureaucracy.

Finally, the late nineteenth and the early twentieth century up to the Depression and the election of Franklin Roosevelt saw the expansion of the merit system to cover more and more positions. This expansion was mainly if not exclusively a presidential issue as lame ducks sought to protect their appointees from removal by the next president.

Emergence of the
Politics/Administration Dichotomy

Early civil service reformers were united by the need to take corruption out of administration, but few gave much thought to how to reconcile the power of an unelected civil service with the political goals of American democracy that placed, at least in theory, the primary responsibility for making policy in the hands of electorally accountable policy-making officials such as Congress and the president. Early reform legislation through the 1880s also had ignored the respective roles of career and noncareer employees or high level presidential appointees in the new regime. This oversight partly reflected the limited scope of the early merit system. If only a handful of clerks and low level employees held tenured positions, their ability to influence government policy in a democracy was hardly at issue. Yet as more and more positions were covered, and as higher level positions were also included under the merit system, the policy-making political power of the civil service grew and threatened the power of elected officials.

The ideological impetus for neutral competence can be traced to late nineteenth century civil service reform movements that were directed at rooting out the corruption and spoils that had emerged in Andrew Jackson's time and which fully blossomed during Lincoln's and Grant's administrations.

The experiences of foreign regimes offered later nineteenth and early twentieth century Americans a model for civil service reform. Woodrow Wilson, writing in his 1885 "Notes on Administration," argued that "the task of developing a science of administration for America should be approached with a larger observance of the *utilities* (Wilson's emphasis) than is to be found in the German or French treatment of the subject."[2] In this essay Wilson stated for the first time that "*administration* should be subservient to the *politics*," (Wilson's emphasis), a distinction that he would make more forcefully in his now famous 1887 essay "The Study of Administration."[3]

The aim of Wilson's two essays was to advocate a science of

public administration and to delineate a distinction between politics and administration. According to Wilson, a science of administration would make government more businesslike and purify its organization.[4] Administration is a field of business that is removed from the "hurry and strife of politics."[5] Administrative questions, for Wilson, are distinct from political questions because while political questions are policy questions, public administration is simply the "detailed and systematic execution of public law."[6] Overall, in borrowing from Biuntschli and other German writers, Woodrow Wilson argued that administration was the detailed execution of general government policies and "lies outside the proper sphere of politics." Policies should be set by elected leaders and their appointees. Administration is the province of politically neutral, permanent officials selected for their expertise.

Wilson's distinction implied the need for bureaucratic efficiency and the existence of general principles of administration that were applicable in both liberal and authoritarian political systems. These management principles sought to drive a wedge between the power of a bureaucrat and that of an elected official and their appointees. Wilson stated that "if I see a monarchist dyed in the wool managing a public bureau well, I can learn his business methods without changing one of my Republican spots."[7]

Though Wilson's essay had little influence until decades after his death,[8] Frank J. Goodnow's 1900 *Politics and Administration* was perhaps the most influential book upon early twentieth century administrative thinking. It sought to clarify the various functions of the state which he described as politics and administration. Politics is defined as the "expressions of the state will" while administration is the "execution of these policies."[9] However, while these are distinct functions, there is a need for a harmony between the expression and execution of the law because a popular government must be able to control the execution of the law if its will is to be expressed. Yet, while politics should control administration, there is a limit to how much politics should penetrate into administration lest the latter become inefficient.

The spoils system had produced a coordination of politics and administration, yet the spoils had two glaring deficiencies. One, it led to the impairing of administrative efficiency. Two, and far more important for Goodnow, the spoils was a threat to popular government and competitive elections because it supported the ruling party and kept it in power. The spoils system, a consequence of strong political parties and a decentralized administrative system, was a threat to democracy because

> the party in control of the government offices had made use of them not merely to influence the expression of the popular will, but to thwart it when once expressed.[10]

While Goodnow did recognize the importance of political parties in a popular government and sought to strengthen them in America, he rejected party (political) control over administration as the best way to harmonize the expression and execution of the popular will. Goodnow rejected perhaps the hallmark Jacksonian defense of spoils that it sustained strong parties and democratic control of the bureaucracy. Moreover, Goodnow also repudiated earlier claims that open competitive exams would end this corruption because these exams were a small part of the reform movement. The solution to preventing administration (party control of offices) from thwarting the political will was to remove it from political and party control.

> That it (popular government) shall not be lost in our case, depends very largely on our ability to prevent politics from exercising too great an influence over administration, and the parties in control of administration from using it to influence improperly the expression of the public will.[11]

The best way to assert a new harmony between the expression and the execution of the laws would be by creating a hierarchial and centralized administration with the president at the head to direct the operations of the government. Such a centralized system with superiors overseeing subordinates would limit the discretion of the latter and, thus, prevent them from acting politically.

While this model of organization sought to subordinate administration to politics, this subordination did not mean that politics should control administration. Instead, Goodnow makes it clear that this type of control is inefficient. There is a certain area of administration that should be insulated from politics. These areas include the administration of justice; technical, scientific information gathering; as well as purely administrative (personnel?) management issues.[12] These functions should be performed by politically neutral, tenured and competent individuals who are to act in a semi-scientific, quasi-judicial, and quasi-businesslike fashion.[13] Such efficient behavior would only be upset by politics.

Finally Max Weber's writings on bureaucratic power in *Economy and Society*[14] were published after his death in 1920 and reiterated themes found in Wilson and Goodnow. Weber described the ideal type of bureaucracy as the technically most efficient type of organization for performing tasks.[15] In appealing to the language of efficiency, Weber argued that administrative organization, if it were to be efficient, must be hierarchically organized and staffed by technically competent experts enjoying life tenure. Moreover, civil servants would be subject to appointment by superiors, but these superiors would be removed from the direct supervision of the bureaucratic functions and tasks.

Central to the arguments of Wilson, Goodnow, and Weber, then, was that politics and patronage threatened the efficiency of administration and that, in general, administrative and political questions were and should be distinct. The former should be addressed by technically competent civil servants insulated from politics. Thus, in these writings we see the emergence of a neutral competence ideology that stressed a politics/administration dichotomy in order to promote efficiency and limit the threats parties posed to popular government. The best way to augment the relationship between politics and government and to ensure that there was a coordination between the popular expression of the public will and its execution was through a centralized and hierarchial organization controlled from the top down. Weber, like Wilson and Goodnow, then presumed the existence of a responsible political center or apex to the bureaucratic pyramid residing in elected officials.

In sum, articulation of a politics/administration dichotomy was meant to preserve political direction by elected policy makers while enhancing government integrity and expertise. Yet an important part of the crusade, particularly on the local level where most of the public sector existed, was a direct attack on political parties and the belief that the proper relationship between party, administration, and popular government was forged by the spoils system. Instead, the reformers believed that spoils damaged administrative efficiency and popular government and did little for the health of parties. Spoils, then, had to give way to the more important goals of technical expertise, administrative competence, and efficiency.

Overall, efforts to depoliticize the civil service and to distinguish between policy-making and non-policy-making officials were grounded in attempts to reconcile bureaucratic power with the values of American representative democracy. Reforms sought to instill the value of neutral competency in the federal government as a check upon abuses of bureaucratic power that came from parties dominating the administration of government.

Judicial Enforcement of the Politics/Administration Dichotomy

The president and Congress were not the only players in the battle to reform the federal bureaucracy. Whatever changes they sought ultimately faced potential challenges in court. Hence, the federal judiciary had an opportunity to shape the debate and direction of reform.

The Supreme Court jumped on the bandwagon of civil service reform quickly and even before the Pendleton Act was adopted several Justices were articulating the language of neutral competence in their decisions. *Ex Parte Curtis*[16] and *United States v. Wurzbach*[17] represent the earliest decisions by the Supreme Court to enforce political neutrality and limits upon financial and campaign activity within the federal bureaucracy. Notable in both decisions, but especially in *Curtis*, is the appeal to a neutral competence logic that rejected spoils and party control of government. However, unlike later cases where First Amendment issues were paramount, in neither of these cases were First Amendment claims crucial legal issues surrounding government restrictions upon political assessments and financial contributions.

Curtis addressed the constitutionality of an 1876 Act that prohibited all members of the executive branch who had received Senate confirmation from "requesting, giving to, or receiving from, any other officer or employee of the government, any money or property or other thing of value for political purposes." Punishment for the above was a misdemeanor and a fine not to exceed $500. Curtis was a federal employee who was convicted of violation of this Act in district court for receiving money from employees. He appealed, contesting its constitutionality.

Chief Justice Waite wrote a majority decision that upheld the Act. First, Waite argued that it was not a complete ban on the political solicitation of money for political purposes. He read it as only preventing federal employees from giving or receiving money from one another. The Act left open the possibility that nonfederal employees or personnel could give money to individuals covered in this Act. Specifically, the Court left in place most types of political assessments and other *legal* graft when it stated that the "managers of political campaigns, not in the employ of the United States, are just as free now to call on those in office for money to be used for political purposes as they ever were."[18] The Act for the Court simply prevented political superiors from demanding that subordinates unwillingly contribute.

The Court did not base its decision of the First Amendment rights of workers (as many of the later Hatch and patronage decisions would). Instead, the Court decided the case on the scope of the powers Congress had under Article I, section 8 (the necessary and proper clause) and asked if this Act went beyond the bounds of proper legislative discretion. In holding that Congress did not exceed its discretion the Court first cited a variety of laws and rules that had been adopted since 1789 that placed some limits upon federal employees accepting money for political purposes. Two main arguments were employed by the Court when inquiring into the legislative purpose of this Act.

First, the Court held that its primary purpose was to promote the efficiency, integrity, and proper discipline of the federal service. Limits upon forced contributions frees workers from the fear of dismissal and thus promoted more efficient performance of duties. Second, the Court argued that a forced contribution system would serve to "furnish indirectly the money to defray the expenses of keeping the political party in power that happens to have for the time being the control of the public patronage."[19] The Court, while noting the importance of political parties to republican government, also deferred to Congress and the contention that party control of the federal service was often dangerous to popular government when that control sought to prevent fair competition and when the party used the government to serve its own needs.

Significant was the language of the two main points of the Court's analysis of the Act. One part of their decision was an appeal to the goals of administrative efficiency and political neutrality that the limits on contributions would serve, while the other was an appeal to the fear of party dominance of the government. Both claims in many ways echoed the rhetoric of the emerging neutral competence movement in their attack upon the spoils system and in damage that spoils caused to a politicized administrative system.

Wurzbach was a 1929 decision that questioned the constitutionality of a 1925 Corrupt Practices Act that made it illegal for officers and employees of the United States to promote their candidacy or reelection in a party primary. Justice Holmes upheld the Act, contending that Congress could provide measures that would limit the political pressure that employees might face to contribute money if they were to retain employment. While Holmes's argument is brief, it also implicitly appeals to a neutral competence ideology in recognizing the need of a politically neutralized bureaucracy.

Wurzbach, in many ways, rested upon a logic similar to his opinion in *McAuliffe v. New Bedford*[20] where Holmes had argued that public employees "may have a constitutional right to talk politics, but

...no right to be a policeman." In making the distinction between a right and privilege to public office, Holmes contended that occupying a public office was no more than a privilege and therefore one had no right to public office. Hence, certain rights, including those to engage in some political activities, may be curtailed in the interests of promoting reasonable control over government employees. The *McAuliffe* right/privilege distinction, as well as the dismissal of First Amendment rights in this decision and *Wurzbach* served as a response to Bradley's dissent in *Curtis* and set the ground for the Court's future willingness to place limits upon the First Amendment rights of public workers in order to promote political neutrality.

Overall, these early decisions defined the terrain for future Court approaches to politics in the federal bureaucracy. There was an appeal to the logic of efficiency, the fear of party dominance of the government, the need to insulate civil servants from political pressure if they were to perform their duties, and the claim that federal employment was merely a privilege such that First Amendment rights could be limited to the needs of administrative control. All these points were made by Wilson, Goodnow, and Weber, and they became important dicta in the rhetoric of neutral competence.

The Progressive Era War Against Politics

While Woodrow Wilson's essay had little influence until decades after his death. Dorman Eaton, head of the New York Civil Service Reform League, Theodore Roosevelt, and F.J. Goodnow were more successful in arguing the need to keep politics and administration apart.[21]

Articulation of a politics/administration dichotomy sought to preserve political control by elected policy makers while enhancing government integrity and expertise. Yet an important part of the crusade, particularly on the local level where most of the public sector existed, was a direct attack on political parties. "Once admit that it is proper to turn out an efficient Republican clerk in order to replace him with an efficient Democratic clerk, or visa versa," wrote Teddy Roosevelt in 1890, "and the inevitable next step is to consider solely

Republicanism or Democracy, and not efficiency, in making the appointment."[22] Reformer and academic Andrew White charged that cities were being governed under the "evil theory" that the city was a "political body." Instead, the city should be considered a corporation where "party political names and duties" were "utterly out of place."[23] Similarly, in 1894 the *Nation* stated of local administration:

> In any other business, occupation, or enterprise but that of city government, a man who should...declare that nothing would induce him...to put a Democrat or Republican in a place for which he was eminently fit, would be treated as a lunatic and confined in an insane retreat by sorrowing friends.[24]

Certainly, George Washington Plunkitt and other machine leaders understood and felt threatened by the attack on patronage and parties, seeing it as an assault on democracy itself. Party bosses expressed concern that, if the common man gets neither job nor favor for political activity, it would be difficult to secure volunteers to work on campaigns.[25]

Some intended the reforms of the era to limit the power of the lower classes, just as opponents of spoils had always held a dim view of widespread participation. Indeed, businessmen in many cities favored replacing election by ward with at-large election, partly because only well-off businessmen were generally able to gain the money and visibility to run a city-wide race. This could and in many cities did shift the composition of government in the first two decades of the twentieth century toward a more pronounced middle-class, business-orientated direction that stressed efficiency, productivity, and other economic or marketplace values.[26]

Emphasis on professional and economically efficient public bureaucracies reflected Progressive beliefs in education and the appeal to technical solutions to solve public problems. Following the institutionalization of such specialized professions as law, engineering, medicine, and accounting, the Progressives saw government as a business that then (and to a great degree even now) was centered around the delivery of basic services.[27] For the Progressives, professionalization meant economy and efficiency and devising the best methods and procedures to perform specific functions and deliver certain services. Professionalization also meant development of new standards and tools to measure productivity, and these standards and tools were provided by the scientific management movement in the early twentieth century.

Taylorism and the Rise of Scientific Management

During the early twentieth century the nature of American business practices changed as companies grew in size and needed new management techniques to increase productivity and personnel control. Businesses were urged to develop long range plans, something relatively few did at the time. More importantly, businessmen were urged to employ trained engineers and others to study the actual work conducted on the factory floor. By using "time motions studies" or observing and timing the motions of workers and eliminating those motions unnecessary for production, managers could find the "one best way" of completing any task with the overall goal of maximizing efficiency.

Thus scientific management, or Taylorism, which was named after Frederick Taylor[28] who performed the first time-motions studies, was quickly embraced by Progressives and it had important social as well as technical influences upon how business and government were run. One result was to encourage bureaucracies to apply scientific management principles to civil service administration, but it also tended to shift power and status from elected officials to the educated, middle-class technocrats they employed because these individuals had technical expertise and knowledge of government operations that the former lacked.[29]

Scientific management had important implications for the structure of organizations as well as for the actual work conducted within. Just as there was one best way of doing any task, there was to be one best organizational structure for all activities, and in the coming decades considerable research sought the perfect span of control and number of levels of hierarchy. Not surprisingly, the systematic study of organizations was quickly embraced by Progressive political reformers.

Reformers were disturbed that the election of honest politicians had not arrested corruption and inefficiency. Indeed, numerous reform politicians were elected without any clear idea of what to achieve once in office, including how to manage the new, larger governments set up by patronage-oriented politicians. Thus, "the old intuitive approach of 'throwing the rascals out' and electing new officials failed ...[since] the new officials had no training, no understanding of 'management,' no supporting staffs. They obviously needed more than honesty."[30]

Hence, efficiency was replacing honesty as the main value driving civil service reform.[31] New university curriculum provided the organizational theory and knowledgeable personnel to improve government management. College and university involvement in public policy was championed by Progressives, and on the state level it originated in LaFollette's Wisconsin. Staff from the University of Wisconsin's Legislative Reference Service provided expertise for Progressive legislative proposals and earned the ire of conservative opponents. Yet when a conservative finally won the governorship in 1914, he found that Legislative Reference Library professionals really were impartial: they left political decisions to their elected masters. The new governor continued to use the agency he had previously denounced to reform the state bureaucracy.[32]

Not surprisingly, Progressive reformers maintained the existence of one best type of government organization, and it bore striking resemblance to Prussian forms. Reformers generally favored regular, monopolistic bureaucracies staffed by careerists and organized according to function. Professionalism and economies of scale assured efficiency and eliminated the waste and confusion associated with duplication or overlapping missions. Separate units of government were not to overlap within the same territory, and the division of power was not to be employed on the local level and might even be questioned on the national level.

"Government by the efficient" was ushered in by the 1906 founding of the New York Bureau of Municipal Research.[33] This private organization was funded by wealthy philanthropists, employing talented academics to develop and promote better means of municipal management. This was the forerunner of similar institutions in Philadelphia, Cincinnati, and several other cities, as well as a national research bureau which eventually became the Brookings Institution.

Both Republicans and Democrats wanted to build and maintain road and sewage systems, and the technologies employed in such service provision were relatively easy to quantify and provide systematically. The quantification and measurement of tasks explain the rapid adaptation and considerable success of bureaucratization, and of the city manager system, which was proposed by reformers in 1909 and first practiced in flood-ravaged Dayton in 1913. City managers were private, nonpolitical experts contracted by the city council for a fixed term to manage city affairs. Early city managers were usually trained engineers reluctant to take stands on controversial issues.[34] Other Progressive administrative reforms including executive budgeting quite successfully improved local government tax collection, administration, and basic service delivery. Well-organized, professional city bureaus also paved and maintained roads, developed water systems, and fought disease.

Besides the University of Wisconsin, other universities began to develop courses, majors, and even schools of public administration as counterparts to those in business administration.[35] These institutions gave reform (and often machine) executives needed expertise, and helped institutionalize Progressive administrative tenets including: rationality, planning, specialization, quantitative measurement, "one best way," standardization, bureaucratic structure, and of course, political neutrality in the federal bureaucracy.[36]

In the wake of successful Army personnel practices employed during World War I, efficiency ratings and testing became "a new near-science" (which was indeed the intent).[37] In fact, the Army became the first large organization of any kind, public or private, to develop and employ a "personnel-classification" scheme, testing members' aptitudes and assigning them accordingly. The system worked fairly well and was widely copied in other federal agencies.[38]

By 1930, these classifications had "become the core of public personnel administration," which was once and for all effectively depersonalized. By Hoover's administration, efficiency and government as a business were the guiding ideologies of American public administration.

Civil Service Expansion from Chester A. Arthur to FDR

The Progressive concerns with efficiency and neutral competence, though important, were mainly ahead of late nineteenth century administrative ideologies. The era of reform symbolized by the Pendleton Act sought to place good, or at least competent people in the civil service.[39] Yet American merit reforms were at least partly conceived in the self-interest of reformers and politicians. Indeed, some reformers recognized this and Carl Schurz in 1871 suggested that a one-term executive could remove incentives to build a spoils machine.[40]

The civil service took permanent root through a combination of ideals, practical need, and political interest. The Pendleton Act initially covered only about ten percent of Federal employees, mainly Washington clerks, and postal and customs officials in urban areas where the complaints of merchants and strength of moralist reformers were most pronounced.

Over a thirty-year period civil service coverage expanded radically through two processes. First, coverage was incrementally extended among government workers in one-party regions not vital to electoral control, and those in positions where expertise was badly needed. Examples of the latter included weather bureau scientists and Indian Affairs teachers and doctors. Similarly, the scientific and technical staff constituted a small (under five percent even in 1900) but rapidly growing proportion of the early civil service.[41] Federal regulation of the private sector made civil service expertise more important in the Progressive era than before, thus adding pressure to protect these technical positions through a merit system.[42]

Second, presidential blanketing in of political appointees into the civil service system, mainly by lame duck administrations, greatly increased the size of the civil service. As a lame duck, President Arthur extended the civil service to about twelve percent of federal employment, thereby saving the jobs of many Republicans who might not have survived the first Democratic administration in twenty-four years.

Grover Cleveland had attracted much support from reformers. Yet as the first Democratic president since before the Civil War, he removed about half the unclassified service in his first eighteen months. After that he doubled the percentage of workers covered by civil service laws from about twelve percent to nearly one-fourth of the government service, suggesting an effort to protect his newly appointed Democrats from Republican and congressional control. However, only two percent of the federal service was converted while Cleveland was a lame duck, perhaps evidence of a genuine desire for reform on his part. President Harrison disappointed reformers. He converted only five percent of the federal service to the merit system, and four-fifths of these came after he had lost the election to Cleveland. In his second term, Cleveland tried to limit patronage abuses and massively increased civil service coverage to nearly fifty percent of the federal work force.[43]

After Cleveland, spoils was not a dominant national issue[44] and the Democratic Party was captured by Jacksonian spoilsman William Jennings Bryan. Once elected, William McKinley did not strongly support civil service reform. Presidential appointees were for the most part competent, and McKinley was the first to limit the removal authority of government managers, but under the influence of various spoilsmen the president actually reclassified several thousand positions from the merit service to political appointment. Logistic errors and scandals under the political leadership of the Army in the Spanish-American War, however, pressured McKinley to tighten management, and helped lead to Roosevelt's nomination as vice president.[45]

Teddy Roosevelt

Given his background, it is hardly surprising that Theodore Roosevelt became the equal of Cleveland in his support of merit reforms. He was the first president since Polk who either "understood or cared much about administration as we think of it today."[46] He wanted to build a strong civil service not only for good government, but also because strong executive bureaucracies could increase presidential power.

Roosevelt advocated a strong presidency able to do anything not specifically prohibited by the Constitution.[47] Roosevelt limited government-employee participation in politics, by forbidding participation in conventions among other things. He also strengthened the Civil Service Commission, introduced a gag rule for executive branch employees, and reorganized some departments partly for efficiency, but also to break up the links between executive employees and congressional committees.[48] Such linkages, known today as subgovernments, then as now, are often powerful coalitions that teamed up with interest groups to make policy, and they often undermine presidential authority.

While most of his appointees were good and loyal administrators, the president was hardly above using patronage to gain support in Congress and divide his opponents.[49] For example, the drastic extension of the merit service under Roosevelt was concentrated in regions already safely Republican. In contested locales, an effort was made to appoint competent Republicans.[50] Despite compromises with political reality, by the end of Roosevelt's presidency, approximately sixty percent of federal employees were fully under the merit system, and another seven percent or so were under some controlled selection system, such as the military.[51]

Roosevelt also set up the Keep Committee to improve the operation of government. This body recommended a government pension system, a central purchasing bureau, and many minor changes in administration, including the economies of window envelopes for mailing, to foster efficiency. Most were eventually accepted.[52]

William Howard Taft

President Taft's appointments were not of the same quality as Roosevelt's, partly because he was determined to make peace with old-guard spoils Republicans who had turned against the Progressives. Yet Taft also expanded the civil service somewhat, even attempting to put government attorneys under some form of merit selection. By the end of Taft's term, approximately seventy percent of federal employees were under some form of merit system, though many of these were blanketed in by the lame duck leader.[53]

Far more important was Taft's quest for efficiency in government. Taft commissioned administrative-reform expert Frederick Cleveland to suggest innovations, and later chose a committee led by Cleveland and Goodnow. Though loosely patterned after the Keep Committee, Taft lavished on it far more attention. Along with many minor management proposals, the body recommended extending the merit service to all non-policy jobs, reorganizing agencies by purpose, and most importantly, creating an executive budget.

While many of the minor administrative proposals were soon adopted and saved a great deal of money, reorganization and executive budgeting threatened congressional-committee links with government agencies, and were stoutly resisted by both bureaucrats and congressmen. Ignoring Congress, Taft instructed federal managers to prepare an executive budget in his last year, but few complied.[54]

Taft's love of efficiency reflected both the spirit of the Progressive Era and the rapidly increasing federal expenditures. The national government ran deficits in four of the six years before 1909, and a greater federal role and size demanded more systematic management.[55] Yet far more was going on. Nineteenth-century business and management ideologies had emphasized hard work, punctuality, calculation, and perseverance, while discouraging systematic study or scholarly discourse. It was not uncommon to find in business magazines with such titles as "Why I Never Hire Brilliant Men."

Factory owners had rejected the overly quarrelsome (and innovative) intelligent employees and instead made good use of the hard-working, docile, dull, and mediocre. This began to change with Taft. By 1900, years of agitation by businessmen had shifted the focus of many colleges and universities from the moral development favored by ministers to a more vocational emphasis.[56] More vocational colleges, along with a proliferation of business colleges and journals, found and preached Frederick Taylor's scientific management doctrine.

Woodrow Wilson and World War I

Extension of civil service laws did not end demands for spoils. When Woodrow Wilson became the first Democratic president since Cleveland, the usual throngs of office-seekers descended on Washington. At first, the president refused to even acknowledge the requests. But soon after taking office Wilson gave in to the pressures of Democratic congressmen and such spoilsmen as Secretary of State William Jennings Bryan in order to safeguard his legislative program. Outside of the State Department relatively few officials lost their jobs, partly because there simply were not very many unprotected positions left.

This angered many spoilsmen. Vice-President Thomas Marshall, for example, remarked that "If there is any office under the government which a Democrat can't fill I believe that office should be abolished."[57] Others disagreed and his statement was widely condemned. For his part, Wilson largely stayed above the fray, though he did purge the Civil Service Commission, staffed new agencies outside the merit system, and proposed no new extensions of the system. The slight extensions which did occur came only after Republican attacks on spoils in the 1916 elections.[58]

But 1913 was to be the last year before the Depression in which federal positions were widely sought, mainly because few positions were available and federal pay was not particularly high. With few political followers on the federal payroll, politicians had less incentive than before to increase salary levels.[59] While the government was well ahead of the private sector in protecting and systematically testing its career employees, it fell behind in compensation. The position of federal employees was gradually improved by an increased demand for government workers and a wave of unionization in the years during and just after World War I.[60] Prior to this wage struggle, employee unions had a few successes. For example, Roosevelt and Taft each tried to make dismissals for cause easier to obtain, and each was in turn rebuffed when unions played on congressional jealousy of its institutional power over administration.[61]

Perhaps partly because of low salary levels, the prewar federal government was neither as expert nor as professional as might be supposed. Preparations for World War I demanded both the rapid expansion of and the import of expertise from the private sector, and the federal government was not equal to the task. To overcome this, Commission rules were relaxed to allow for rapid growth, and many technical specialists were hired directly from companies or universities without examination. Often scientists and managers were given temporary appointments for the duration of the war. Fortunately, patriotism led many affluent experts to take newly authorized uncompensated ("dollar a year") positions to patch together adequate wartime administration.[62]

The Era of Normalcy

Not surprisingly, the 1920 presidential race had little to do with civil service. Once elected, President Warren G. Harding appointed a very mixed group of officials and allowed them considerable autonomy. Some, most notably Commerce Secretary Herbert Hoover, respected the rights of careerists who honestly administered their organizations. Others did not, resulting in Teapot Dome and other scandals.

Though certainly more honest than many of his men, Harding himself showed little respect for the merit system. Like other presidents, he staffed new positions through patronage hirings.

Harding went further, at least once abolishing a few dozen merit positions and then reestablishing them and hiring loyal Republicans.[63] Harding's actions were not wholly those of a spoils politician. Contemporary political appointees might sympathize with Harding's Labor Secretary Davis's who complained that "I am powerless to enforce changes which I desire because I am powerless to put in charge of these places individuals in sympathy with these changed policies."[64] Still, there was no wholesale raid on Washington and the disruption was in fact far less than in 1913.

Seeking to make up for his predecessor's errors, President Calvin Coolidge fully respected the merit system, increased its scope, and based his political appointments almost completely on competence and ideology. Herbert Hoover used the same appointment criteria and further extended the merit system to cover eighty percent of Federal employees. By this time, very few of the remaining twenty percent could be considered endangered by political change.[65]

Along with the strengthening of the merit system, the Era of Normalcy produced various administrative developments advancing toward a more centralized and coordinated national administration run by the executive. The Classification Act of 1923 set up regular compensation schedules. More importantly, as both commerce secretary and president, Herbert Hoover fought to reorganize government in a Progressive fashion to end duplication and concentrate like functions within the same organizations. Hoover admitted that reorganization was unlikely to save much money. Rather, it would enable government to complete its tasks more effectively and efficiently, doing more with the same rather than the same with less.

Hoover thus accepted the modern concept of efficiency as getting the greatest per unit output for input, in essence, the greatest social utility. Congress and the mass public, however, generally saw efficiency as economy (saving money).[66] Promises to disrupt traditional subgovernments without significant economies held little appeal for congressmen, and the proposed reorganizations of 1921-32 accordingly never gained much support.[67]

Far more important as a reform during this era was the actual adoption of an executive budget. The weight of wartime deficits accomplished what Taft's best efforts could not. Seeing a need for frugality, Congress passed the 1921 Budget and Accounting Act establishing a regular process for the executive branch to develop and present a coordinated annual budget to Congress. The Act also set up the Bureau of the Budget (BOB) as the president's chief accountant and the General Accounting Office as its congressional counterpart. The BOB, now known as the Office of Management and Budget (OMB), quickly developed a reputation for careful, economy-driven analysis that it retains in some circles to this day.

Conclusion

From the passage of the Pendleton Act in 1883 until the Depression and the end of Hoover's administration, civil service reform underwent several changes as presidents both extended the merit system to cover more and more federal positions, and as presidents adopted Progressive Era values that placed a premium on promoting organizational efficiency. These changes, especially the latter in emphasizing economy, efficiency, and expertise, transformed the ideology of reform from rooting out corruption to promoting efficiency. The overall goal of this era was to professionalize the federal bureaucracy and to render it more technically competent by rendering it politically neutral.

Efforts to depoliticize the civil service and to distinguish between policy-making and non-policy-making officials were grounded in attempts to reconcile bureaucratic power with the values of American representative democracy. Reforms sought to instill the value of neutral competency in the federal government as a check upon abuses of bureaucratic power. These checks were meant to distinguish administration from politics.

Despite the various attacks on and adaptations to the politics-administration dichotomy over the last ninety years, it continues to hold attraction to some political appointees and high-level careerists. While all agree that a strict distinction is impossible, trying to maintain careerist subordination and limited responsibility can be seen as part of a long-term symbiosis pairing careerists with stability and political appointees with the ability to get things done. As a political appointee explained over 30 years ago:

> ...if we need professionals to staff these positions, we also need men who develop a certain defensiveness in seeing that career people do not become excessively involved in political matters. There is a certain legal fiction in this whole area. We have to hold to it, or else we would be right back to the spoils system. If we did not have this myth of the nonpolitical professional administrator, we would be close to disaster. We cannot staff all the political positions required by the administration. If we are going to keep the government running, we have to live the myth and propagate it.[68]

Notes

1. Hofstadter 1955 and Goodwin 1978 offer good accounts of the history of the Populist movement in America.

2. Wilson 1968b: p. 49.

3. Wilson 1968a: p. 359.

4. Wilson 1968: p. 363.

5. Wilson 1968a: p. 370.

6. Wilson 1968a: p. 372.

7. Wilson 1968a: p. 379.

8. Van Riper 1958 notes how Dorman Eaton, head of the New York Civil Service Reform League, Theodore Roosevelt, and F.J. Goodnow more successfully argued the need to keep politics and administration apart. Later, Max Weber and others clarified the distinction between politics and administration.

9.   Goodnow 1967: p. 18.

10. Goodnow 1967: p. 131.

11. Goodnow 1967: pp. 131-132.

12. Goodnow 1967: p. 78-82.

13. Goodnow 1967: pp. 85,87.

14. Reprinted as "Bureaucracy" in Gerth and Mills 1979.

15. Gerth and Mills 1979: p. 214.

16. 106 U.S. 371 (1882).

17. 280 U.S. 397 (1929).

18. *Ibid.* p. 373.

19. *Ibid.* p. 375.

20. 155 Mass. 216 (1892).

21. Van Riper 1958: pp. 478-479; Schiesl 1977: pp. 74-76.

22. Schiesl 1977: p. 39.

23. Schiesl 1977: p. 8.

24. Schiesl 1977: p. 46.

25. Riordon 1963: pp. 11-16.

26. Schiesl 1977: pp. 134-144.

27. Mosher 1982: pp. 71-72.

28. Taylor 1911.

29. Hofstadter 1955: pp. 243-244, 255; Hofstadter 1964: pp. 257-258, 262-264.

30. Stone and Stone 1975: p. 20.

31. Mosher 1982: pp. 70-79.

32. Hofstadter 1964: pp. 199-204.

33. Mosher 1982: p. 67.

34. Schiesl 1977: pp. 171-181.

35. Stone & Stone 1975: pp. 20, 28-36; Schiesl 1977: pp. 112-126, 131.

36. Mosher, 1982: pp. 72-73.

37. As Van Riper notes, the Army became the first large organization of any kind, public or private, to systematically develop and employ a "personnel-classification" scheme, testing members' aptitudes and assigning them accordingly. The system worked fairly well and was widely copied. Van Riper 1958, p. 252.

38. Van Riper 1958: p. 252.

39. Mosher 1982: pp. 64-70.

40. Hoogenboom 1961: p. 100.

41. Van Riper 1958: p. 161.

42. Skowronek: 1982, pp. 71-72.

43. Van Riper 1958: pp. 117-132.

44. The same cannot be said on the local level. In many cities late nineteenth and early-twentieth-century elections pitted reformers

against spoilsmen, and some local machine politicians themselves came to adopt merit examinations and other reform innovations. Schiesl: 1977.

45. Van Riper 1958: pp. 170-177; Skowronek 1982: pp. 113-118.

46. Van Riper 1958: p. 179.

47. Arnold 1986: p. 24.

48. Skowronek 1982: pp. 178-186.

49. Van Riper 1958: pp. 181-184. The president was also not above using the Secret Service to spy on opponents. Skowronek 1982: p. 187.

50. Skowronek 1982: pp. 178-179.

51. Van Riper 1958: pp. 202-203.

52. Arnold 1986: pp. 25-27; Van Riper 1958: pp. 190-191.

53. Van Riper 1958: pp. 213-215; Skowronek 1982: p. 193.

54. Arnold 1986: pp. 40-51.

55. Arnold 1986: pp. 26-29.

56. Hofstadter 1964: pp. 240-241, 256-260.

57. Van Riper 1958: p. 238.

58. Van Riper 1958: pp. 228-239, 271-272; Skowronek 1982: pp. 195-198.

59. Van Riper 1958: pp. 245-246.

60. Van Riper 1958: pp. 273-281.

61. M. Nelson 1982: pp. 766-767.

62. Skowronek 1982: pp. 200-203; Van Riper 1958: pp. 255-264.

63. Van Riper 1958: pp. 285-287.

64. Van Riper 1958: p. 287.

65. Van Riper 1958: p. 289-296.

66. This modern definition of "efficiency" was also employed a decade earlier by academic Frederick Cleveland in his work under President Taft. Arnold 1986: pp. 36-37.

67. Arnold 1986: pp. 64-82.

68. Bernstein 1958: p.48.

Chapter VI

The Civil Service under
FDR and the New Deal

Introduction

To many, the presidency of Franklin D. Roosevelt was a major watershed in American politics and history. His presidency, coming at the time of the Great Depression and during World War II, ushered in tremendous changes in terms of the role of the federal government in the regulation of the economy. For some, the New Deal represented a major constitutional moment or revolution in terms of defining presidential and national power, especially in terms of how the power of both grew in contrast to the authority of Congress and the individual states.[1]

But FDR's presidency also had a significant impact upon the civil service and the structure of the federal bureaucracy, although at first glance one might not recognize that impact. At the start of the Roosevelt presidency the civil service was well on the way to being substantially covered by the merit system under an administrative system significantly controlled by congressional legislation. It was also a civil service system aimed at rooting out the evils of spoils. Similarly, by the end of the Roosevelt presidency the same could also be said of the civil service, yet, in between, the federal bureaucracy was vastly transformed in size, the merit system appeared savaged, and charges of presidential patronage and spoils dictated fights among the president, Congress, and the Supreme Court for control of the federal government. Overall, the "federal civil service of the nineteen thirties presents a study in contrasts. At first the disintegration of 50 years of experience seemed almost complete; but by 1940 an astonishing degree of order had appeared on the scene."[2]

The presidency of Franklin Roosevelt permanently altered the way the federal service was organized. The changes pushed through by the New Deal and World War II created a powerful presidency that redefined many of the basic assumptions of our constitutional and political order, yet in the end the basic premises of merit hiring and neutral competence remained in place.

Hoover, the Depression, and the Civil Service

Black Tuesday and the stock market crash in October, 1929, interrupted an almost fifty-year period that had produced the gradual depoliticization of the civil service through presidential extension of the merit system that included eighty percent of the federal employment by 1932. Throughout the 1920s, and especially during the Hoover administration, reforms sought to modify and improve classifications of federal positions. These reforms also sought to make salary adjustments and to standardize duties across similar positions. The gradual extension of the merit and classification systems by each president to more and more positions demonstrated that the reform movement had succeeded and that the old spoils and patronage system was now in disrepute. Under Hoover, a former engineer, Progressive goals were also accepted, with the president aiming to reorganize the federal bureaucracy to make it more efficient.

On October, 29, 1929, the stock market crashed and lost over forty percent of its value.[3] That crash started the Depression and the greatest economic collapse in American history. To get a basic idea of the severity of the extent of the Depression, from October, 1929, until November, 1933,

> ...the number of units of manufacturing enterprise had dropped from 133,000 to 72,300; production had declined nearly 48 per cent; and industrial income had declined from $29,000,000,000 to $2,900,000,000.

The condition of labor was only a reflection of this situation. Of the workingmen normally employed in the nondurable-goods industries 26 per cent were out of work; of those employed in the durable goods industry 51 per cent were out of work...Between 1929 and 1933 labor income had declined from $51,000,000,000 to $26,000,000,000—a drop of 48 percent.[4]

Real weekly earnings dropped an average of thirty percent, total weekly man-hours worked per week had dropped by 1932 by sixty percent, and estimates of the overall unemployment rate in the country ranged from twenty-five to forty percent, representing a total of fifteen-million unemployed in addition to those underemployed.[5] Tens of thousands of family farms were repossessed or closed by banks because of severe agricultural crises stemming from over production and cheap farm prices. Even banks, and insurance and finance companies were closed as millions of depositors made "bank runs," demanding to have their money back. On the more individual level, many formerly middle-class families were forced to hit the road, beg, or live in shacks or shanties called Hoovervilles.

Hoover's initial response to the Depression and stock market crash was not to create new government programs to help people. He pleaded and begged with business not to cut production or lay people off. He did not initiate a public works program or support government- sponsored food shelves, or any other types of programs to help people. This was not out of a lack of compassion so much as the business view that unemployment and the Depression were being prolonged by malingering and unionizing.[6] Hoover did encourage the states to cooperate with the private sector to come up with programs to help people. Insisting that "Prosperity was just around the corner," he mainly sought to talk up the economy and inject optimism into the business community. Eventually, late in his term Hoover did suggest such programs as the Reconstruction Finance Corporation (RFC), which aimed at reinvestment and reconstruction of the business sector.[7] By that time Hoover's political support was weak and his actions were widely viewed as uncaring or insufficient.

Surprisingly, the Depression had little effect on the civil

service. The classification and merit systems were not scaled back and surprisingly, neither was government employment despite attempts to cut the federal deficit to balance the budget. From 1929 to 1933 federal employment increased from 579,559 to 603,587. Only 100,000 positions were not classified by 1930,[8] and these were at all levels of federal employment. Classification and reform were not seen as impediments to the government's response to the Depression. They were still depicted as efficiency and reform measures. Thus, despite the Crash and the emerging Depression, it was business as usual for the reform movement and the merit system. However, one event changed all that, the election of Franklin Roosevelt in 1932.

FDR, the New Deal, and the Transformation of Patronage

> *"You can forget all of us. All you have to remember is one name: Roosevelt."*
>
> *Adam stared at him. "Roosevelt?"*
>
> *"Sure. F.D.R. Nobody else but. Because he's the man, sport, who really put the skids under your uncle, and he did it several years ago."*
>
> *"I don't get that at all," Adam said. "Why Roosevelt?"*
>
> *"Because," Jack said patiently, "He destroyed the old-time boss. He destroyed him by taking away his source of power...The old boss was strong simply because he held all the cards. If anybody wanted anything—jobs, favors, cash—he could only go to the boss, the local leader. What Roosevelt did was to take handouts out of the local hands. A few little things like Social Security, Unemployment insurance, and the like, that's what shifted the gears, sport. No need now to depend on the boss for everything; the Federal Government was getting into the act."[9]*

During Franklin Roosevelt's first administration, the merit system was under attack as the president expanded tremendously the size of the federal bureaucracy and filled those positions not according to a merit classification system, but with patronage and individuals who ideologically agreed with him. But by 1940, the civil service system was again used; almost the entire bureaucracy was covered by merit classification, and a new public administration ethic organized the federal bureaucracy. How did this change come about?

When FDR first took office in 1933 he was the first Democratic president since Wilson. This created pent-up demand for new office seekers, and in 1933, prior to FDR taking office, a book was compiled listing the 100,000 positions which were not classified and which could be filled through patronage. FDR, through James A. Farley, his postmaster general, proceeded then to develop one of the greatest patronage hiring systems in American history. Such hiring, needless to say, was condemned by civil service reform leagues and Republicans.

The return of patronage in government was not the end of Roosevelt's assault on the merit system. As part of his response to the crisis of the Depression, FDR had created by 1934 over sixty new agencies that were meant to address the problems of the economy. Most of these agencies, known as the "alphabet agencies" because of the use of letters of the alphabet as abbreviations for the agencies' names, were enacted by Congress, often without deliberation, during the first 100 days of his administration.[10] Among the new agencies created were the Securities and Exchange Commission (SEC); Agricultural Adjustment Administration (AAA); Farm Credit Administration (FCA); Civilian Conservation Corporation (CCC); Federal Emergency Relief Administration (FERA); Public Works Administration (PWA); and the Tennessee Valley Authority (TVA). These agencies, and dozens of others, were created to encourage economic development, put people back to work, and to create fair labor standards and practices that would encourage business competition. In the process of creating them, federal employment shot up from 603,000 in 1933 to 867,000 in 1936 and almost 900,000 by the end of FDR's first term. With federal employment increasing so rapidly, hiring practices were not always consistent and often varied by agency, with some following procedures more carefully than others. Merit classification and hiring did not follow this rapid increase in the civil service, and by the end of 1936 only sixty percent of the federal positions were covered. This was the smallest percentage in thirty years, and this increase in federal employment gave the president significant ability to hire over 400,000 patronage employees.[11]

The type of patronage ushered in during this era differed from that of earlier times since it was essentially ideological and intellectual: Roosevelt sought to recruit those most sympathetic to his policies and programs. This contrasted with earlier patronage which stressed party loyalty first and almost exclusively. Of course, this intellectual patronage upset many Democrats, but more importantly, it achieved an ideological revolution in the federal government. The president was able to recruit individuals who shared his beliefs that a competitive, individualistic, laissez-faire economy could no longer work and that a government-business partnership was essential to turning around the American economy.[12] The first New Deal, or the New Deal programs up until 1936, represented a major intellectual change in how Americans viewed the economy and it gave the president enough political control over the government to bring about its structural transformation.

While this ideological revolution appeared to enjoy significant popular and private-sector support, the Supreme Court was resisting it. This was a Supreme Court packed with conservatives and defenders of laissez-faire capitalism. They were very skeptical of the constitutional status of the alphabet agencies, the scope of the commerce and regulatory power these new agencies had, and the delegation of rule-making power to private business groups to create business standards and practices.[13]

Starting in 1935, the Supreme Court issued a series of decisions including *Schechter Poultry v. U.S.*, *Panama Refining Company v. Ryan*, and *Carter v. Carter Coal Company*,[14] among others, that effectively struck down as unconstitutional most of the first New Deal programs. The claim of the Court was both that the federal government had not justified its constitutional role in regulating some forms of commerce that seemed to have little burden on the national economy, and that there were limits to how far Congress could delegate power to the president and then the president to private groups. As the Court stated, delegated power is not delegable.

The scope of these decisions rendered many of the alphabet agencies powerless. But in addition, these decisions, along with *Humphrey's Executor v. United States*,[15] drew sharp new limits on presidential removal power and control over the federal bureaucracy. In 1926 in *Meyers v. United States*,[16] former president and now Chief Justice Taft wrote for the Court and invalidated the 1876 Tenure of Office Act. This Act, which had required Senate approval before the president could remove an appointee the Senate had confirmed, was declared to be an infringement on presidential administrative control. Yet in *Humphrey's*, the Court drew a limit to presidential power, invalidating an effort by Roosevelt to fire someone from the Federal Trade Commission (FTC) because of policy differences. Stating that the FTC was meant to be non-partisan and removed from direct political and presidential control, the Court appeared to affirm the value of neutral competence and in the process draw a line as to how far Roosevelt could go in his use of patronage and spoils. Hence, the Court appeared to have had the last word in the new change in the American government.

However, the 1936 landslide reelection of Roosevelt over Alf Landon, and the president's 1937 Court Packing Plan to replace aging and conservative justices appeared to give new sanction to the president's agenda. In the wake of the Court-striking down the first New Deal, the Roosevelt administration came back in 1936 with the second New Deal reforms and alphabet agencies very similar to the first.[17] However, unlike *Schechter*, et al., the Court upheld the second New Deal by both distinguishing these programs from the earlier ones it had invalidated, and by essentially repudiating its earlier laissez-faire ideology.[18] By 1937, the Court had begrudgingly accepted the New Deal and the new public philosophy and role of the government.[19] Within a few years, FDR managed to appoint enough justices sympathetic to his views to end fear of future Court challenges.

Presidential Reorganization and the Brownlow Commission

Throughout FDR's second term during the late 1930s, the size of the federal government continued to grow as both New Deal programs expanded and, especially after 1938, the federal government started to add civilian personnel in defense-related areas as military conflict in Europe heated up. From 1937 until 1941, civilian employment in the federal government increased by over seventy percent, jumping from 895,993 to 1,437,582.

With this continued expansion of the size of the federal government, two new problems emerged. One, the size of the federal government had made the existing management structures inefficient because the new government was quite complex and there was no real hierarchy to give the president control. The president needed to do something to institutionalize his reforms otherwise a subsequent president or Congress could destroy the alphabet agencies and remove all those patronage positions he had filled. Two, by 1936, a popular backlash had developed against his massive use of patronage and now there were some demands in Congress (mostly from Roosevelt's critics) and in the press that something be done, lest the return of corruption and spoils of the old days.

The president's response to the first set of problems was to move toward an executive reorganization of the federal bureaucracy. By 1936 Roosevelt was finding coordination of the various New Deal agencies cumbersome. He was ripe for advice even as Louis Brownlow, a leading public administration scholar with Progressive Era roots, had been organizing a study of the executive for two years. Even if the president was not prepared for such advice, Virginia Senator Harry Byrd was beginning to show interest in Brownlow's work. Meeting with Brownlow, Roosevelt became convinced that such a study need not counter his interests, and the president commissioned it after approving the other committee members, Charles Merriam and Luther Gulick. Byrd's congressional committee funded a different study.[20]

The Brownlow Committee report was issued just before the

start of FDR's second term.[21] It began with a rousing call for an executive capable of "vigorous action and leadership."[22] This required a reorganization to put the executive branch in line with the canons of Progressive management, principles which had already been followed in the restructuring of several governorships. Among the committee's more important recommendations were: expansion of the White House staff; placement of the managerial agencies of government, particularly the Bureau of the Budget, under more direct presidential control; extension of the merit system "upward, outward, and downward to cover all non-policy-determining posts"; enhanced compensation to attract better civil servants; reorganization of the existing one-hundred agencies and independent commissions into a more easily grasped number of large departments united by function; and a study of budget and accounting procedures.[23]

The main thrust of committee recommendations was to build the executive into a cleaner, more tightly knit hierarchy differentiated by function, with the president and White House at the top of a thin political layer overseeing highly professional career bureaucrats. "The president needs help," the report declared, and the efficient, clear unity of purpose within the federal bureaucracy as set forth in the Brownlow Report, could provide such help.[24]

In the short term, Roosevelt's power was waning and Brownlow bore little fruit. The opposition of Senator Byrd and other New Deal opponents in part was premised upon the belief that the Brownlow Report and presidential reorganization were aimed at further consolidating Roosevelt's power.[25] Joining congressional critics in opposing the bill, the Brookings Institution argued that the president should not have a near monopoly on administrative power.[26] Hence, the 1937 executive reorganization bill was killed.

Only later, in 1939, did Congress pass an act enabling the president to employ several White House assistants. The Act also permitted limited reorganization authority. FDR immediately used this authorization to mold the Bureau of the Budget and several much less important planning agencies into the Executive Office of the President (EOP).[27]

The merit system coverage was also enlarged, but this

reflected other factors. Merit was by now fully accepted. In 1934 the League of Women Voters launched a very successful state and local effort to limit patronage and extend the merit system. Two years later Republican presidential candidate Alf Landon attacked the administration's bypassing of the system. By that time the New Deal expansion of government was over, so there was no reason not to blanket in the mainly pro-Roosevelt administration to ensure that the president's men could not be removed and the New Deal reforms scaled back. Merit expansions occurred through executive order and the Ramspeck Acts of 1938, 1940, and 1943. By World War II, well over ninety percent of federal employees were under some form of merit system. Personnel organs were set up in the departments and personnel practices were tightened, all with the intent of institutionalizing Progressive reforms, Brownlow recommendations, and merit system principles.[28]

The Hatch Act

As a result of congressional and popular reaction to Roosevelt's blatant use of patronage, new fears that the president would politicize the federal bureaucracy emerged. With over forty percent of the civil service not covered by the merit system, FDR had tremendous control over whom he could appoint. Congress, after Roosevelt attempted to purge New Deal opponents from the Democratic party in 1938, feared that the president would use his appointees to continue his attacks against them. A series of laws were passed placing numerous restrictions upon the political activities of government workers. While previous reforms, such as the Pendleton Act, had supposedly done this, these new laws closed loopholes and extended the political ban well up the executive hierarchy.[29]

These 1939 laws were known as the Hatch Act[30] and this Act was in many ways a Progressive Era reform that placed limits on the political activities of federal workers including bans upon running for office, campaigning for others, and fund-raising or soliciting funds.[31] Violations of these prohibitions were to be enforced by the Civil

Service Commission (CSC) through dismissal or other sanctions. The long term effect of the Hatch Act was in building up an insulated (if not neutral) administration.

Passage of the Hatch Act was denounced by some who contended that it violated the First Amendment free speech and associational rights of government workers. As a result, the constitutionality of the ban on political activity was attacked in court. In 1947 in *United Public Workers v. Mitchell*, the United States Supreme Court upheld the Hatch Act.

United Public Workers grew out of a complaint by several members of a federal union who desired to engage in political activities including acting as poll watchers and serving as ward chairman, which had associated with it a variety of duties including distributing literature, organizing rallies, and hanging political banners. While much of the first part of the *United Public Workers* addressed standing and jurisdiction issues that are not of concern here, the second half of the decision addresses the merits of the Hatch Act.

Justice Reed gave the opinion for the Court in a 4-3 decision. His opinion was joined by Burton and Vinson, with Frankfurter offering a separate concurrence. Justices Black, Rutledge, and Douglas dissented. Reed opened up his opinion for the Court by addressing the First Amendment challenge that the Act is an unconstitutional restriction upon federal employees' free speech rights to engage in political activity. The Court confronted this claim head on by stating that human rights are not absolutes and that "the interference with free expression is seen in better proportion as compared with the requirements of orderly management of administrative personnel."[32] Several factors contributed to the need to limit the political activity of workers in order to promote good administrative management.

First, the Court noted how if political activity of federal workers hurts the civil service, its damage is no less if the activity occurs after work hours. Second, the Court indicated how free speech rights had to be balanced against the need to protect a democratic society against the evils of political partisanship in the federal service.

Specifically, the Court, in citing public administration scholarship as authority,[33] argued that there was a need to limit political activity in order to promote "political neutrality for public servants as a sound element for efficiency."[34]

Elsewhere, the Court also noted how an "actively partisan governmental personnel threatens good administration," and that it would be absurd to think that Congress would not have the power to limit that political activity that is "offensive to efficiency." Finally, the Court stresses that party activity may hurt political neutrality and that, overall, partisan political activity is a threat to efficiency, political neutrality, and discipline.

Black's dissent, as well as the dissents by Douglas and Rutledge, significantly followed the arguments of the Court of Appeals that held that the Hatch Act was overbroad in its scope and in its infringement of the First Amendment rights of workers. Black, for example, argued that the Hatch Act does not help promote clean democratic government but instead disenfranchises millions of individuals. However, Douglas took on the supposed need to separate politics from administration in the federal service by arguing that perhaps it should be the higher levels of the administrative system and not the lower levels that ought to be politically neutralized. His reason for that is that if partisan activity undermines the efficiency and confidence in the bureaucracy, then those who are most beholden to patronage (those in higher level positions) should be limited in their activities. Yet even Douglas, despite his dissent, also cites public administration scholarship[35] on the virtues of political neutrality. His real disagreement seemed to lie not in the majority's appeal to efficiency and the evils of spoils but in the locus of where the neutralization should occur.

Overall, *United Postal Workers* appeared to settle the constitutional controversy surrounding the Hatch Act, but given that the case was decided by less than a majority of the Court, a more definitive answer by the judiciary would have to wait until 1973 when the Court again upheld the constitutionality of the Act in *United States Civil Service Commission v. Letter Carriers.*[36]

World War II

Mobilization for World War II posed many of the same problems confronted during the first World War. As before, it was difficult to process the numerous applicants for federal jobs quickly while still trying to follow civil service procedures. There was also the problem of coordinating and mobilizing the federal bureaucracy toward the single effort of fighting the war. Indeed, these and other problems were in many ways more difficult than in World War I.

First, the civil service in 1940 was far larger than in 1917. From 1941 to 1942, the civilian employment in the government almost doubled, from 1,437,682 to 2,296,384. It reached an all-time high of 3,816,310 in 1945. To try to implement the New Deal while gearing up for war put tremendous pressure on the Civil Service Commission to process even more applicants than in 1917. For example,

> from June 1, 1939, through June 30, 1945, about 8,900,000 placements were made within the executive civil service, the largest number occurring between July, 1942, and June, 1943, and totaling approximately 2,700,000.[37]

This new workload led Congress, which would be ambivalent toward civil service rules throughout the war, to question how effectively and quickly the Commission could act and follow its rules. While War Service regulations did eventually relax some competitive requirements,[38] especially for the difficult-to-fill technical fields, the Commission assured Congress that it could keep up with the workload and no legislative suspension of the rules was necessary. The Commission did manage to keep up but only through a variety of management techniques that delegated some of its power to individual federal agencies.

Second, unlike 1917, by the start of World War II, almost ninety-five percent of the federal personnel were covered by civil service procedures. This contributed in part to the Civil Service Commission's heavy workload, but it also meant that there was far less flexibility for the government to move or transfer individuals around to combat personnel needs in different areas. In addition, the growing specialization of the civil service made it more difficult to transfer because significant training would be needed for placement in new positions that often needed very specialized skills.

Third, the special problems of running a war economy led to labor shortages because workers were needed for civilian defense and non-defense jobs as well as for private-sector employment and the armed forces. Usual surplus pools of educated, trained, and work ready individuals were not available as the national unemployment rate dropped from about twenty-five percent in 1933 to barely one percent in 1944. This led to the significant government recruitment of women and African-Americans who soon accounted for almost forty percent and twelve percent respectively of the civilian civil service by 1944.[39] Women occupied just about twenty percent of the positions before the war and twenty-six percent by 1947; African-American prewar employment amounted to almost ten percent.

Fourth, running a war economy led to problems of centralization and coordination of the federal bureaucracy, with significant defense pressure for the military to run the economy and government. Fortunately, these demands were not met and civilian rule prevailed and sought to balance the economic needs of the government, consumers, producers, and farmers. Numerous specialized wartime economic agencies, such as the Office of Price Administration, Office of Production Management, and the National Defense Advisory Council, among others, were formed to ration consumer items and monitor wages and prices, to ensure that production needs for the war were met and that price-gouging and shortages did not hamper the economy. Challenges to presidential and congressional efforts to maintain price controls were raised in court, but in *Yakus v. United States*,[40] the Supreme Court refused to hear them, upholding a federal law that made it illegal to contest the constitutionality of the price controls until after the war was over.

Moreover, centralization of the federal bureaucracy beyond even those reforms suggested in the Brownlow Report was required in order to meet war-time needs. By way of a 1942 executive order, the War Manpower Commission (WMC) was created to coordinate employment needs in the federal government. The Civil Service Commission, never more than a legislatively-created executive support service, was forced into a subordinate role below the WMC and was entrusted with the civilian employment needs and allocation in the federal government. In this role, its powers over personnel were never absolute and on at least a few occasions Senator Byrd and others sought to limit its powers and cut civilian employment in the government. One way the CSC dealt with this problem, along with its strained workload and demands for centralization and coordination of manpower allocation, was to encourage and supervise the establishment of personnel departments in many of the federal agencies which undertook their own recruitment, examination, and position classification functions. Obviously, new coordination problems and conflicts with these department personnel agencies developed, but were never really resolved during the war.

Finally, the issue of political loyalty and the concern to keep communists and German or Japanese sympathizers out of the federal service was an item that the CSC had to confront. Anticipating the "Red Scares," Senator McCarthy, and congressional Un-American Activities Committee communist witch hunts of the 1950s, the loyalty issue became an important if perhaps unsubstantiated concern. During the war, the Commission refused to certify for employment individuals who expressed communist or German-American Bund loyalties.[41] The CSC undertook significant evaluation of the federal personnel with over 350,000 individuals investigated for political views from 1939-1945. Concern with loyalty was precipitated by the paranoia of war politics and it led to many tragic results including the property confiscation of over 100,000 Japanese-Americans living on the West Coast and in California, and their forced relocation to detention camps in the Arizona desert. Few real threats to American security were found as a result of the above investigations. Exclusion from federal employment based on one's political beliefs was unfortunate, and later Court decisions and legislation placed limits on this practice.

Public Employee Unions

One of the more important changes in the civil service during the New Deal and Roosevelt era was the emergence of public employees unions as important political forces in the federal bureaucracy. Public sector unions, such as those for postal carriers, were around from 1863. They had some early twentieth century political influence on wage demands as a result of the Lloyd-LaFollete Act of 1812 that gave federal workers the right to organize and petition Congress for grievances. Not until the New Deal did public employee receive much recognition. This was because section 7a of the 1933 National Industrial Recovery Act (NIRA), in conjunction with the Norris-La Guardia Act, had given private employees the right to organize and join unions without employer threats or interference.

Although the NIRA and eventually the Wagner Act did not sanction or apply to public employee unions, it had a ripple effect encouraging their formation.[42] From the 1920s through 1945 several different federal public employee unions emerged with shifting affiliation with either the American Federation of Labor (AFL), the Congress of Industrial Organizations (CIO), or as independent unions such as American Federation of Government Employees (AFGE). Since World War II numerous other unions and affiliations have emerged with most (approximately sixty percent) of the civil service now unionized.

Public employee unions during the Roosevelt years were instrumental in organizing to establish collective bargaining for wages and benefits and in devising grievance procedures to protect union members against arbitrary treatment or infringement of civil service regulations. Congress and the executive branch gave some recognition to both practices after the war, but not until the Kennedy administration did federal employee unions really start to grow and collective bargaining become more of an accepted practice. However, even today the rights of these unions remain open, and their ability to negotiate for wages and salaries is nil.[43]

Public-sector unions never really had the same rights as

private sector unions. This is especially true regarding the right to strike. While unions did receive much support from Roosevelt, he did not support their unlimited rights to strike and stated as early as 1937 that the rights of the state to serve the public were superior to union demands.[44] As a result, during the war, strikes and boycotts were avoided by the federal unions.

In 1947, section 305 of the Taft-Hartley Act banned public employees from striking.[45] In fact, no union did try to strike until 1981 when PATCO (Public Air Traffic Controllers) and the federal air traffic controllers went on strike after the Reagan administration had dragged its feet in negotiations over working conditions and wages. Subsequently, Reagan fired all striking controllers and had PATCO decertified. Despite this anti-union action, public employee unions remain important in the federal government and they have served an important function in protecting workers' rights and preventing political favoritism and spoils from interfering with the hiring and organization of much of the federal government.

Conclusion

The civil service and the organization of the federal government under Franklin Roosevelt is a study in contrasts. At the start of FDR's administration in the Depression there was a social ethic supporting a small limited government as well as some signs of the resurgence of spoils. By the end of World War II there was a reinvigorated economy with a much larger and interventionist government that was more centralized than before, with civil service regulations, unions, and a more activist judiciary protecting most if not all federal personnel. While Roosevelt's actions and transformation of the civil service were clearly the result of many external factors, including the Depression and the War, his presidential leadership was important in bringing about the creation of the modern presidency and civil service.

FDR's overall early patronage strategy reflected a wish to use positions to hold the Democratic party together while at the same time rapidly staffing agencies with competent individuals who believed in their organizations' missions. Many academics devised and staffed the New Deal, who for the first time in American history joined government in great numbers. FDR used political patronage to sell policies, but used "ideological patronage" to devise and administer the New Deal, making many new agencies into what David Lilienthal, a product of the system, labeled "a kind of Phi Beta Kappa version of Tammany Hall."[46]

In addition, while Roosevelt initially appealed to spoils to build his government and a Democratic party, one of the president's more enduring legacies might be that he also killed or significantly wounded local party politics in America. By federalizing many social programs, he shifted loyalties away from the local political party and toward the national government. No longer would individuals need to support a local ward boss to receive a job; they could instead turn to some federal bureaucracy for help. Hence, while the Hatch Act politically neutralized federal workers, the New Deal also undercut many of the motivational reasons for individuals to support parties. Hence, the New Deal replaced party politics with administrative politics.[47]

In short, FDR's administration effected both a structural transformation in how the federal government and civil service were organized, and an ideological revolution in attitudes toward the presidency and the role of government in American society. While Roosevelt did make it acceptable for the government to become more involved in social-welfare issues, he also brought a new administrative ideology into the federal government. This ideology, "government by managers," represented the triumph of the Brownlow Committee recommendations, and it recognized the rise of the administrative presidency with strong executive leadership and direction by political elites at the top of the bureaucracy who issued policy directives to theoretically apolitical career civil servants. Government by managers thus represented the perfection of the organizational model of bureaucracy as described by Max Weber and other organizational theorists.

Notes

1. Ackerman 1991.

2. Van Riper 1958: p. 315.

3. Schlesinger 1957: p. 159.

4. Rayback 1966: pp. 320-321.

5. Malone and Rauch: 1960: pp. 536-537.

6. Schlesinger 1957: pp. 178-179; Burns 1985: p. 544.

7. Schlesinger 1957: pp. 238-240.

8. Van Riper 1958: p. 312.

9. O'Connor 1956: p. 299.

10. Leuchtenburg: 1963, pp. 52-60.

11. Van Riper 1958: p. 320.

12. Leuchtenburg 1963: p. 63.

13. Schlesinger 1960, pp. 454-460.

14. *Schechter Poultry v. U.S.* 295 U.S. 495 (1935); *Panama Refining Company v. Ryan* 293 U.S. 388 (1935); and *Carter v. Carter Coal Company* 298 U.S. 238 (1936).

15. 295 U.S. 602 (1935).

16. 272 U.S. 52 (1926).

17. Schlesinger 1960: pp. 385-409.

18. Compare: *NLRB v. Jones & Laughlin Steel,* 301 U.S. 1 (1937); *Mulford v. Smith,* 307 U.S. 39 (1939); *U.S. v. Darby,* 312 U.S. 100 (1940); *Wickard v. Filburn,* 317 U.S. 111 (1942), among other important cases.

19. Lowi 1979.

20. Arnold 1986: pp. 91-95.

21. Brownlow, Merriam, and Gulick 1980.

22. Arnold 1986: p. 127.

23. Arnold 1986: p. 129.

24. Arnold 1986: p. 130.

25. Cook 1996: p. 114.

26. Mosher 1969: p. 81.

27. Arnold 1986: p. 114.

28. Van Riper 1958: pp. 332-343.

29. Van Riper 1958: pp. 339-343.

30. 5 U.S.Code § 7324 (1988). The original versions of the Hatch Act are listed as Act of August 2, 1939, ch. 410, 53 Stat. 1147, and Act of July 19, 1940, ch. 640, 54 Stat. 767.

31. The 1940 Hatch Act extended a similar ban on political activities to state and local workers receiving federal funds.

32. *United Public Workers v. Mitchell*, 330 U.S. 75, 94 (1947).

33. *Ibid.* p. 97, footnote 32.

34. *Ibid.* p. 97.

35. *Ibid.* p. 121, footnote 10.

36. 413 U.S. 548 (1973).

37. Van Riper 1958: p. 374.

38. Van Riper 1958: pp. 369, 375.

39. Van Riper 1958: pp. 377-379.

40. 421 U.S. 414 (1944).

41. Van Riper 1958: p. 396.

42. Dulles 1964: pp. 264-266; Rayback 1966: pp. 320-325.

43. Levitan and Nodeen 1983: pp. 9-10.

44. Van Riper 1958: p. 350.

45. Van Riper 1958: p. 351.

46. Van Riper 1958: p. 327.

47. Cook 1996: p. 107.

Chapter VII

The New Deal Administrative Consensus from Truman to Ford

Introduction

The legacy of the administrative reforms that took place during the New Deal and World War II lasted beyond the time span of these two events and the Roosevelt presidency. In terms of creating a more powerful administrative presidency and federal government there would be little major challenge to the reforms ushered in during the years Roosevelt occupied the White House. From Truman to Nixon, there was little effort to disturb the basic administrative power relations between Congress and the president and there was no real challenge to the goals of civil service reform in terms of continuing to cover more positions by the merit system or otherwise enforcing the values of neutral competence or administrative efficiency.

In part, this consensus was a by-product of the Cold War where a strong presidency was regarded as imperative to fighting communism, and the consensus was also a result of relative stability in the party composition of Congress, with both houses remaining Democratic from the early 1950s until the Reagan administration. Stability in congressional party governance and consensus on Cold War goals precluded presidents, both Republican and Democrat, from seeking any major challenges to a federal civil service that was guided by the pursuit of efficiency, neutral competence, and presidential dominance. Instead, while the broader paradigm of federal administrative organization was unchallenged, efforts to sort out the particulars of the New Deal administrative organization dominated the presidencies of Truman through Nixon. Often, the exact controversies of each presidency reflected the different concerns and policy issues of the times.

Specific issues dominating civil service reform and organization would change dramatically from 1946 through the Nixon administration. In the early post-war years demilitarization of the federal bureaucracy, extension of the merit system, efficiency, pay, and job classification were dominant themes. But as the Truman administration turned into the Eisenhower presidency, and as the fear of communism and the Cold War heated up, the political loyalty of the federal service became a more important issue occupying the attention of the Civil Service Commission.

With Eisenhower, the first Republican in 20 years, patronage and presidential transition again became an issue as new senior level appointees had to contend with lower level officials for control of the federal bureaucracy. Eisenhower's presidency revealed a new twist to the politics-administration dichotomy as the location of line between presidential and careerist power was debated. Not only did the conflict between career and noncareer officials (political appointees) raise questions about presidential control of the bureaucracy, it also sparked questions about the political role and accountability of civil service in American democracy and about how much ideological control a new president should have in directing or redirecting the federal government.

Doubt over the ideological and political neutrality of the civil service and federal bureaucracy became significant in the 1960s as Kennedy and Johnson increasingly used the federal government as a tool to fight poverty and alleviate social ills. The viability of the politics-administration dichotomy was raised, and other questions were asked about the effectiveness of the federal government in securing its objectives and in serving its clients. Liberal and conservative critics articulated different visions of where the federal government should be headed and how its personnel organized. Thus, by the end of the Nixon-Ford Era, issues that had dominated the civil service for the last fifty years, such as extension of the merit system, were replaced or translated more directly into questions about presidential power and the status of the civil service in American politics.

Truman and the Postwar
Demobilization of the Civil Service

The end of World War II brought new problems to the federal government and civil service. In contrast to the early years of his administration, by 1945 Roosevelt had created a federal bureaucracy that was well organized in a hierarchial chain of command with the president and other senior officials making policy and delegating to lower career officials. This was a federal government with 3.8 million civilian workers, over ninety-two percent of them covered by civil service law.[1] It was the epitome of the Weberian and Progressive bureaucratic model, placing strong political leadership at the top and neutral administrators and career civil servants below. However, this was a war bureaucracy and not one directed toward peace.

But as early as 1944 President Roosevelt saw an end to the war and began issuing directives to demilitarize the government and prepare for "normal" peacetime functions. The issue of demobilization would be a major theme and concern of the Civil Service Commission (CSC) during the early postwar years, yet given the many beneficial administrative reforms that had occurred as a result of the war, the CSC was unwilling to abandon them and return to the status quo, much as the government had after World War I. Given the Depression before the war, and the changed state of the American economy and world position afterward, returning the federal government to the days of Taft seemed naive. The American government had a new role in the world and in the economy, and that role demanded the professional and organized bureaucracy that had been created. The CSC, then, had to demobilize, hold on to reforms, yet translate those reforms into the operations of mainly non-defense matters.

Vice-President Truman inherited this situation after FDR's death in 1945. Truman was essentially in favor of the merit system, and made few notable changes except to strengthen the system by adding a few senior Internal Revenue Service (IRS) senior positions to the classification system. He did place in office many of his cronies and supporters, but by the late 1940s there were only 70,000 available patronage positions, shrinking to 15,000 by 1952. By the late 1940s over ninety percent of federal personnel were covered by strict civil service laws that made it extremely difficult to fire or discipline employees. This made political reprisals more difficult, but presidents also claimed that it weakened their ability to control their subordinates and the federal bureaucracy in general. Neutral competence, while laudable, had undermined presidential control, despite the reforms ushered in under Roosevelt.

Loyalty became a larger and larger issue that the CSC had to address. During the war the commission had made over 356,000 loyalty investigations. In 1946 President Truman issued Executive Order 9835 directing all prospective public employees to be checked as security threats. Evidence of this included membership in the Community Party among ninety other private groups the Attorney General had deemed subversive.[2] By 1953, when the order was revoked, 4,756,705 persons had been investigated, with almost all cleared. This intrusion into the First Amendment free association and speech rights of individuals did result in a few hundred dismissals and several thousand resignations in response to investigations.[3]

In addition to presidential loyalty checks, both the House and Senate had Un-American Activities Committees (UAAC) that investigated charges by Senator Joseph McCarthy, Congressman Richard Nixon, and others that the Communist Party and other subversive organizations had infiltrated the federal government, including the State Department. Hearings into these activities often included McCarthy haranguing federal employees about their activities and publicly trying them in the press. While the Supreme Court did place some late restrictions upon these hearings,[4] it later backed down[5] and the 1950s record of the Court in halting the "McCarthy Hearings" and other prosecutions of alleged communists was mixed.[6] Not until the 1960s did these hearings and prosecutions end, and it was only in the 1970s that the House and Senate disbanded their Un-American Activities Committees and the Attorney General's List of subversive organizations was destroyed.

Thus, checks into loyalty, the demilitarization and shrinking size of the federal government, and the changing economic conditions of the postwar 1940s had an impact on the civil service. Partisan congressional investigations of corruption and poor performance in the IRS and Reconstruction Finance Corporation (RFC), problems of low pay, and presidential and McCarthyite probes of disloyalty in the civil service also hurt morale in the Truman era and through the early Eisenhower years.[7]

Finally, the Korean conflict which started in 1950 ended Truman's interest in civil service reform as concern turned yet again to developing employment procedures for remobilization and remilitarization of the federal government. As with the previous two world wars, emergency personnel policies were adopted to expedite hiring and reorganization of the government. Other changes in the bureaucracy included the renewed growth in civilian employment of the federal government, the establishment of separate Defense Department hiring procedures, and the increase in the number of temporary as opposed to permanent appointments to civil service positions. As the Korean conflict ended, procedures for reducing staff and demilitarizing the government and economy had to be implemented.

The First Hoover Commission and the Administrative Procedures Act

The great size and new missions of the permanent federal establishments transformed the career bureaucracy into a serious political actor capable of challenging or limiting congressional and presidential power. Moreover, longstanding Democratic domination of the national government tended to obscure the potential conflicts between political appointees and careerists. Especially under the Truman administration, drawing the line between patronage and career positions was difficult. Hence, reorganization of the federal government was needed, and Truman established the First Hoover Commission (headed by the former president Hoover) to make personnel and organizational changes.

The 1949 Hoover Commission report on executive reorganization hardly mentioned the matter of where patronage versus the civil service line should be drawn. It did make twenty-nine other recommendations. Among the more important ones: establishment of a Commission on Ethics in Government to set ethical standards for government officials and civil servants; development of a comprehensive pay policy that would establish uniform salaries across similar positions and in comparison to private sector equivalents; development of training programs for civilian federal employees; development of new promotional and classification policies making it easier for employees to advance; development of new efficiency ratings to evaluate performance; and decentralization of many of the classification and personnel policies including those for promotion, dismissal, and transfers.

The major thrust of the First Hoover Commission was the decentralization of many government functions and the further development of a professional career civil service. However, the Commission did ignore overseas federal employment, extension of the merit system to new positions, and executive development of senior civil service officials.[8] Ignored also were the political questions of public sector unions, how bureaucratic power fit into American democracy, and if and how bureaucratic personnel should represent the American public. All these were pressing issues that would grow over the next forty years.

As a result of the First Hoover Commission report, numerous changes occurred. The CSC, pursuant to the 1949 Classification Act, reclassified many positions, the Executive Pay Act of 1949 changed salary schedules, and the Performance Rating Act of 1950 simplified and implemented new efficiency measurement procedures. Other reforms were suggested but held up by Congress.

In addition to changes recommended by the Hoover Commission, further unionization of the federal government was also occurring in the organization of the civil service and federal bureaucracy at this time. In 1946 the CSC had established its commitment to a professional civil service and issued a six-point policy statement on this topic. It had promulgated "temporary civil service rules" to cope with demilitarization and the changes in civilian employment, and it also developed programs to push through decentralization of many of its functions.

In 1946, Congress passed the Administrative Procedures Act (APA).[9] The APA outlined the rule-making and adjudicative power of the numerous regulatory agencies that had been created through the New Deal. The APA represented the first major statutory attempt to apply constitutional principles regarding governance and operations to at least part of the federal government. The APA stipulated standards for evidence, hearing procedures, and some public interest representation and participation in the deliberations of regulatory agencies. While far from perfect, the APA was an important first step in opening up the federal bureaucracy to the American political process. Subsequent amendment and Court decisions in the next thirty or so years, along with a change in public administration philosophy in the late 1960s, greatly increased the client service and political accountability of the bureaucracy. Overall, the APA recognized the reality of the large administrative state and it sought to create rules that would bring legal order and regularity to the federal bureaucracy that had been created out of the New Deal and the war.

The Eisenhower Presidency

The 1953 executive transition had a considerable impact on the career service, and one which in many respects anticipated changes later in the Nixon and Reagan administrations. In 1952, the Truman administration blanketed in large numbers of previously noncareer officials. By this time well over ninety-five percent of federal positions were under some sort of merit system, and the new administration had only about 15,000 positions immediately available for patronage. (Tens of thousands more would become available after fixed terms or when their holders retired or died.)

Fortunately the new president's relative disdain for patronage made this a relatively minor concern. Indeed, many Republican congressmen were disturbed by the relative absence of patronage.

More important to career-noncareer relations was the change in the party of the executive. Less than seven percent of the civil service in 1953 had ever before served under a Republican president.[10] Eisenhower and many of his appointees were reluctant to trust the career bureaucrats who had been hired by and served under twenty years of Democrats. The new president wrote John Foster Dulles that "almost without exception, these individuals reached these high administrative offices through a process of selection based upon their devotion to the socialistic doctrine and bureaucr..ic controls practiced over the past two decades."[11]

Though personnel relations under Eisenhower varied widely from organization to organization, many political appointees sought to dominate policy through hiring and reductions in force (RIFs). This was particularly true in domestic organizations. Indeed, save for Draconian security checks, particularly in the State Department, owing to McCarthyite pressures, the foreign policy and defense bureaucracies were relatively untouched.[12]

Given longtime stability and the expectations it built up, the attacks on domestic organizations damaged already weakened morale. This was particularly true in such organizations as the Rural Electrical Administration and the Housing and Home Finance Administration, where the political appointees selected to run the agencies actively opposed their missions.[13] In these and certain other organizations, the new appointees used mass transfers to encourage some executives to resign, making room for new, "politically correct," to use today's term, officials.[14]

The administrative effectiveness of Eisenhower appointees may have been enhanced by careful efforts to foster unity and teamwork among the top political appointees, including regular Cabinet meetings to preach cooperation. The Cabinet's relative ideological and social homogeneity made this possible. Because the long political exile left few Republicans with national executive experience, Eisenhower tended to seek former governors and successful businessmen who focused on efficiency and who considered government inferior to the private sector.[15] In his first year, Eisenhower also moved to increase and formalize the numbers of political appointees at high levels in government by inaugurating the new and highly controversial "Schedule C" personnel classification for "positions of a confidential or policy determining character." Eisenhower's reclassification provided needed political leadership for the sprawling New Deal and foreign policy bureaucracies, and differentiated top level career bureaucrats and policy makers from lower level and more administrative-type civil servants.[16]

In 1953 a Second Hoover Commission Report recommended a more strict delineation between policy making and administrative decisions. It suggested the development of a "senior civil service" of several thousand top careerists who could be moved around as management and political concerns dictated. These ideas were largely forgotten until the President Carter's 1978 Civil Service Reform Act created the Senior Executive Service.[17]

Better remembered, at least in public administration circles, were Norton Long's arguments in favor of representative bureaucracy.[18] In the manner of Jefferson's equal division of offices, Long argued that the power of administrators over policy was inevitable. A pure dichotomy was not possible. The bureaucracy should not be controlled by the executive so much as it should be ideologically diverse. In this way, it could represent the nation in policy making, perhaps better than the elected branches could.[19] Long's ideas, while ignored in the 1950s, would become important in the late 1960s and 1970s.

Though career-noncareer civil servant/appointee relations started badly in the Eisenhower administration, initial hostility could not last. By the second term, early efforts to prune and control the domestic bureaucracies were largely forgotten and interactions were relatively routine, perhaps partly since a basic reorientation of the role of government received little support in congressional elections. Most of Eisenhower's controversial initiatives were by then mainly discarded.[20]

Kennedy

The Kennedy administration's transition into office was smoother than its predecessor's for a number of reasons. First, with Democrats in control of Congress, Kennedy did not face the same party conflict that Eisenhower faced when he became president. Second, the narrow margin of victory, with Republicans actually gaining congressional seats in the 1960 election, kept the administration from attempting dramatic reforms. Finally, the narrow victory discouraged the appointment of ideologues even as the abundance of former Truman and Roosevelt officials allowed the administration to appoint many who had experience in the federal system. These experienced administrators were more in tune with careerists. Perhaps more important was the new president's relative disinterest in bureaucracy, and organization in general. Moreover, the methodical and hierarchial style developed by Eisenhower was by its nature repugnant to the flamboyant Kennedys, who favored a less businesslike structure. Rather than take over disfavored organizations (e.g., the State Department) the Kennedy style was to ignore and bypass them by concentrating power within the White House or developing new organizations such as the Peace Corps to reflect their philosophy.

The most significant action taken by the Kennedy administration vis-a-vis the civil service involved the federal unions. At the urging of his Labor Secretary Arthur Goldberg, in 1962 Kennedy issued Executive Order 10988, which established the right of federal employees to form and join unions.[21] While the Order did recognize some unions, it did no more than establish some informal collective bargaining, and even when bargaining was allowed, the rights of employees were subordinate to the public interest of the agency in which they worked. Unions then, as is true even today, lacked the right to bargain for wages and had to lobby Congress politically for salary changes.

Despite the limited rights that the Kennedy administration gave to unions, his Executive Order 10988 helped spur membership growth in unions from 180,000 in 1963 to 843,000 in 1969.[22]

Johnson and the Great Society Programs

Kennedy's plans and administration were cut short by his assassination on November 22, 1963. With Johnson's ascension to the presidency, and his change in style and temperament, many of the Kennedy appointees left after the 1964 election. While Kennedy himself was no longer president, the momentum of his political agenda was carried over and built upon during the Johnson presidency.

Three themes dominated the ideology of President Lyndon Johnson, all of which would in various ways influence public administration and the organization of the federal service. First, there was the commitment to a war on poverty and the elimination of poverty in America. Prompted by both Kennedy's pledge to helping the poor and by Michael Harrington's *The Other America: Poverty in the United States*,[23] Johnson, in his 1964 State of the Union message, declared an unconditional war on poverty and urged the passage of several bills, including the Equal Opportunity Act of 1964, to provide more income support, job training, and other social welfare services to the poor.

A second characteristic of what came to be known as the Great Society programs was Johnson's commitment to equal opportunity and civil rights for Blacks and other minorities. The clearest statement of this commitment came in a June 4, 1965 speech, at Howard University in which he proposed not just equal opportunity for all, but equal results.[24]

> It is not enough just to open the gates of opportunity. All our citizens must have the ability to walk through those gates...We seek not just freedom but opportunity. We seek not just legal equity but human ability, not just equality as a right but equality as a fact and equality as a result.

A third characteristic of the Great Society programs was the overall belief in the capacity of the government to manage the economy to maintain long-term growth. Great Society economic theory rested upon the success of the 1964 tax cut, which stimulated investment and led to the creation of many new jobs. This tax cut, an example of Keynesian fiscal policy, was paradigmatic of an emerging philosophy that stated that with the proper federal budget adjustments, changes in tax revenue, and income transfers to the needy, well-trained government policy makers could act like technocrats to fine tune the economy for continued economic growth.

The result of these three goals was to usher in the largest non-defense social-welfare-orientated federal growth in programs and government agencies since the New Deal. The Great Society even surpassed the New Deal in budgetary scope and focus. From 1965 through 1974, federal expenditures increased from $37.7 billion to almost $140 billion by earmarking funds in seven areas: income support, health care, low-income housing, education, manpower or job training programs, civil rights, and community empowerment programs for low and moderate income individuals.[25] Among the programs or legislation created or expanded during the Johnson Great Society era were: the 1964 Economic Opportunity Act, Jobs Corp, Head Start, Aid to Families with Dependent Children (AFDC), Medicaid and Medicare, 1964 Civil Rights Act, 1965 Higher Education Act, 1965 Elementary and Secondary Education Act, Housing and Urban Development Acts of 1965 and 1968, and the Voting Rights Act of 1965, among other programs. Many of these programs still exist despite their recent scaling back by Reagan and other administrations, and they clearly had a profound influence upon the organization of the federal government.

The most direct effect that the Great Society had upon the federal service was to increase federal civilian employment from 2.5 million in 1965 to over 3 million by the time Johnson left office in 1969. While some of the increase could also be attributed to the gearing up of the government for the Vietnam War, most of the increases were in Great Society programs. This growth in civilian employment created job opportunities for many and it required the Civil Service Commission to classify many hundreds of thousands of new jobs and prepare competitive exams, such as the PACE test, for entry level employment into the government.

The Great Society was not the only issue to dominate the

Johnson or later the Nixon administration. The Vietnam War and the eventual growth of American forces to over 500,000 in that country strained the American economy. Yet Johnson and many of his advisors did not see a conflict between running the Vietnam War and implementing the Great Society.[26] Johnson felt that "guns and butter" could be paid for without any tax increase or sacrifice, yet the only way that could be accomplished was through deficit spending. Efforts to try to build up the social welfare and military effort without tax increases at a time of nearly full employment was a recipe for economic disaster and it led many to question either the efficacy or desirability of the Great Society programs, or to rethinking the basic concepts of public administration and the organization of the federal service. The result was the split into right- and left-wing critics, creating the New Public Administration movement.

New Critiques of Public Administration

The Great Society's efforts to manage the economy yet find ways to best serve client needs, Kennedy's disdain for bureaucratic structures, and the creation of unconventional and very non-bureaucratic federal programs such as the Peace Corps were precursors of later 1960s attacks on the federal bureaucracy. The attacks came chiefly from two very distinct groups: radical academics, and conservative (neoliberal) theorists and politicians. From the center and left, new critiques of bureaucratic organization and the New Public Administration movement assaulted the conventional bureaucracies and the politics-administration dichotomy. From the right and center, intellectuals had long assaulted the ability and integrity of public bureaucracies, and their views were largely accepted and at times implemented by Presidents Nixon, Reagan, and to some degree Carter.

The 1960s began with great promise, but they were not happy times for the field of public administration. There were fewer soul-searching articles in the top public administration journals than in the previous decade that lamented the lack of professionalization or organization in the federal bureaucracy. At the decade's beginning, many fully expected government bureaucrats to act like technocrats to manage the economy, abolish poverty and social pathology, and use public resources with unprecedented efficiency through such new tools as Planned Program Budgeting (PPB). Unfortunately, the Great Society's conflicts with the Vietnam War, and the realization that the war on social ills was more than merely a technocratic problem, led to a questioning of the role of government and the civil servant in the federal bureaucracy.[27]

Organizational and public administration theorists argued that the increased size, complexity, and rapid change of modern technologies forced public and private organizations to discard old bureaucratic forms for less hierarchical, more consensual, and more rapidly changing organizational forms.[28] Such organizations would have to consider the goals of members as well as the organization's, and work hard to integrate the two if the agency or bureaucracy were to secure its mission. Emerging new organizational critiques, coupled with the disappointments of the Great Society public administration theorists, led some into radical new directions.

The New Public Administration movement was born out of the above conflicts and reflected a questioning of traditional public administration assumptions. Meeting at Syracuse University's Minnowbrook retreat in September 1968, several important public administration scholars, including Dwight Waldo, H. George Frederickson, and Frank Marani presented papers and discussed the state of the public administration discipline. Among the conclusions reached were: social equity, in addition to efficiency and economy, should be of concern to administrators; ethics and honesty should be paramount concerns of public officials; agencies must grow, change, or wither away to reflect the needs of clients and social problems; hierarchial organizations should be challenged with the focus not upon rational structures but upon the best way to serve client needs; and effective public administration should be defined in context of an active and participatory citizenry.[29]

The Minnowbrook scholars forcefully argued that public administrators needed to reject traditional bureaucratic structures that suffocated the authority they represented. New public organizations must be fluid and consensual. More importantly, the old-fashioned politics/administration dichotomy was no longer a viable distinction since it failed to consider the goals of equity, equality, and participation that changing social conditions demanded.

Public administration and its practitioners should not be value neutral since this would merely reinforce the positions of the powerful. Instead, public administration should promote equity and social change, no matter the positions of those in official authority.[30] Administrators should be more representative of the interests of the American public they served if the federal bureaucracy were to be both effective and accountable to the values of American democracy. Naturally, this value-oriented autonomy could and did in fact give civil servants considerable power beyond that ceded by elected officials.

The result of the New Public Administration movement was felt in several ways. One, attempts to make the composition of the bureaucracy more socially representative of the American public were initiated through the help of affirmative action programs that started under the President Johnson. These programs were both the result of policies adopted by the CSC and of Court decisions later in the 1970s that encouraged a more diverse and representative civil service. Two, management practices in the federal government changed to reflect new employee relations. These changes included new receptivity to unions, collective bargaining, employee participation in management decisions, and the articulation of new grievance procedures and employees' rights.[31]

Three, through self-initiative and eventually through numerous Court orders, federal agencies, especially regulatory agencies, opened up their decision-making process to more citizen participation. For example, in *Goldberg v. Kelly*, the Supreme Court mandated that administrative hearings must grant clients due process before terminating or changing benefits.[32] *Goldberg*, as well as other decisions that expanded the legal doctrine of "standing," or the right to bring a case in court, led to the creation of formalized rules and procedures that allowed aggrieved or interested parties to challenge the decisions or decision-making process of agencies.

Overall, the Minnowbrook conference and of the recommendations of the liberal New Public Administration scholars had a significant impact upon the organization of the federal bureaucracy. They sought to integrate better the civil service and servant into American democracy by making both more socially accountable and representative of the American public. Many of these issues, including a concern for equity, have become institutionalized as part of the organization of the federal government.[33]

Conservative Critiques

Very diverse, and often right-wing critiques of public service and the New Public Administration movement emphasized the increased disenchantment with the performance of public institutions at all levels of government. Theodore Lowi argued that this was the inevitable result of expecting too much of the national government, particularly the president, and of empowering interest groups and professionals at the expense of parties.[34] By enlarging the role of government while weakening the political parties, the modern state assured domination by interest groups and subgovernments who were able to assume greater control over the policy-making process of the government.[35]

Though they shared Lowi's distrust of subgovernments, other conservative critics of the Great Society Programs emphasized different factors.[36] They argued that the design of government institutions and selection of which government services to provide in a liberal society must take into account the individual incentives of those both in and outside of government. While these authors generally addressed local service delivery, many of their comments were relevant to the federal government as well. In particular, many argued that bureaucratic civil service systems undermined government accountability and ability to provide needed services by removing clear responsibility and incentives for good performance. This belief led to a variety of rather old-fashioned prescriptions, including the call for a return of spoils or the use of economic incentives to keep bureaucrats and bureaucracies in line.

Additionally, some criticized the entire New Public Administration movement as immature and illogical.[37] Victor Thompson assailed attempts at making the bureaucracy more socially accountable and demographically descriptive of the American public as a threat to representative government and as a perversion of traditional notions of merit and equality. Attempts to make the bureaucracy more "compassionate" not only undermined bureaucratic efficiency, but they complicated decision making and made government action more difficult. The result of the efforts to humanize, politicize, and decentralize the bureaucracy would not be to improve government service but make it more costly and cumbersome. The upshot of the comments by Thompson, Lowi, and others was that the Great Society was flawed and the New Public Administration movement was misdirected. Both needed to be changed, and the Nixon administration offered a chance to do that.

The Nixon-Ford Years

Unlike the more liberal supporters of the New Public Administration, conservative reformers had a chance to implement some of their ideas in Washington in the 1970s and 1980s as political appointees in the Nixon and Ford administrations, and later in the Reagan administration.

The Nixon transition was in many respects similar to that of Eisenhower's sixteen years before. Like Eisenhower, Nixon was a conservative who questioned a strong federal role in domestic affairs, in rhetoric if not in fact. Nixon inherited from Johnson a federal establishment which had grown considerably, with new functions fighting poverty and greatly increasing aid to states and localities. He also inherited the Vietnam War defense establishment. Nixon had little clear idea, at least at first, of exactly what he wanted to do with or to the federal establishment or how to deal with the Vietnam War, despite his 1968 campaign promise that he had a secret plan to end it.

Unlike Eisenhower, Nixon won election by a razor-thin

plurality rather than a large majority, and he lacked the previous Republican's political and administrative skills. At first Nixon, to a greater extent than his predecessors, appointed a diverse Cabinet and allowed it considerable leeway in developing policies, perhaps partly because of the initial absence of a domestic agenda. Due to a liberal Congress and public opinion, albeit in a smaller way, he also continued the Great Society expansion of a federal role, creating such new organizations as (Occupational Safety and Health Administration (OSHA) and the Environmental Protection Agency (EPA). Yet these progressive agencies, as well as most of the Great Society bureaus, did not agree with the president's basic political predispositions. For example, he warned his Cabinet that

> if they did not act quickly, they would become captives of the bureaucracy they were trying to change...We can't depend on people who believe in another philosophy of government to give us their undivided loyalty or their best work...If we don't get rid of these people, they will either sabotage us from within, or they'll just sit back on their well paid asses and wait for the next election to bring back their old bosses.[38]

Nixon's early Cabinet-style government did not last long. Though Nixon wanted his Cabinet members to be independent, he was soon disappointed with just how independent they could be. In the absence of a clear agenda, these officials tended, quite naturally, to pick their own teams and push the objectives of their departments. Nixon had always planned to run foreign policy directly from the White House, but had hoped to leave domestic policy and the Cabinet to its own, presumably Nixonian devices. When the Cabinet predictably went in many Great Society focused directions, Nixon reconsidered and increasingly centered domestic policymaking in the White House. This was manifested in three ways.

First, Nixon developed plans for administrative reorganization to center authority in several supercabinet positions in close touch with the White House. This transparent power grab could not pass Congress, though to a very small degree power was centralized through the reorganization and politicization of the old Bureau of the

Budget, now the Office of Management and Budget (OMB). More importantly, by the middle of the first term an increasingly enlarged and differentiated White House began to take a greater role in policy-making. This proved unworkable. The White House lacked the organizational capacity to do the work of the departments, and was unable to work its will.

Finally, in the latter part of the first term, elaborate plans were laid to reorient White House personnel practices. Rather than dominate policy through the White House, the president would instead use White House personnel organs to place conservative political appointees in subcabinet and lower positions throughout the administration. Efforts would be undertaken to transfer or otherwise neutralize a particularly troublesome careerist. The "Malek manual" on use of the personnel system, prepared by a Nixon appointee in HEW who came to direct the White House Personnel Operation in 1970, was notable in this regard.[39]

The impact of the Nixon bureaucratic reforms is debatable. Some feel that his administration was enfeebled by the Vietnam War, his paranoia, opposition in Congress and the bureaucracy, and Watergate before it could carry most of its plans to fruition.[40] Still, Nixon was successful in using ideological tests as a means of getting many conservative Republicans into high level career positions, thus replacing many of the more liberal Kennedy and Johnson holdovers.[41]

Nixon was also successful in slowing down the Great Society initiatives through gradual reorganizations and rewritings of regulations in the early 1970s that gave political appointees more power, particularly in social welfare policy. Nixon stonewalled Congress and used a variety of executive delaying tactics, including impounding congressionally appropriated funds, to kill or limit many programs he did not like. Eventually, the 1974 Congressional Budget and Impoundment Act drew limited the president's ability to impound or redirect funds.

The Court Revisits the Hatch Act

In 1947, *United Public Workers v. Mitchell* upheld the Hatch Act, but only by a four-vote plurality. This margin left open what a full Supreme Court would decide, and in 1973 a 6-3 decision supported the Hatch Act's constitutionality.

United States Civil Service Commission v. National Association of Letter Carriers (*Letter Carriers*) was a challenge to Section 9 of the Hatch Act. Here, six members of a union desired to campaign for candidates for public office. Part of their challenge to the Act was to question the vagueness of Section 9 that banned "political activity." The other part of their claim was to argue that decisions subsequent to *Mitchell* had eroded its holding such that the First Amendment rendered the ban on political activities unconstitutional. The Court rejected all these claims. What should be noted is how *Letter Carriers*, like *Mitchell*, appealed to a neutral competence rhetoric to defend its arguments.

The majority rejected patronage and stated that "federal service should depend upon meritorious performance rather than political service, and that the political influence of federal employees on others and the electoral process should be limited." The basis of this claim rested in the majority's recounting the nineteenth century reforms directed against spoils and in their agreement that "partisan political activities by federal employees must be limited if the government is to operate effectively and fairly." Political neutralization is a must if representative government is not to be eroded by the will of a party taking control of the government. Elsewhere in their decision, the Court appealed to the language of efficiency and the importance of political neutrality to the good performance of administrative duties as other reasons why the Hatch Act imposed reasonable restrictions upon the First Amendment rights of federal workers.

In a brief dissent, Justices Douglas, Brennan, and Marshall make two arguments that would justify overturning the Hatch Act ban on political activity. First, the meaning of the Act's restriction that no one shall take "an active part...in political campaigns" was so overbroad and vague that it lacked legal precision. In noting that the Civil Service Commission's own rulings on this prohibition were voluminous, the dissent claimed that it would lead to a chilling effect upon the exercise of free speech among federal employees. The second claim was that *Mitchell* was no longer good law because that decision rested upon the logic that government employment was a privilege, not a right, and therefore employment could be conditioned upon the sacrifice of certain rights. Instead, the dissent noted that recent decisions, specifically *Perry v. Sindermann*,[42] had eroded that right/privilege distinction. Limitation of one's First Amendment rights could not be a condition for federal employment, especially if the requirements in the Hatch Act were not narrowly tailored and precise to the activity prohibited.

In upholding the Hatch Act in 1947 and 1973, the Court placed its stamp of approval upon the neutral competence as an important goal of public administration. The Court's rationale in upholding the Act clearly appealed to the rhetoric of neutral competence, including the language of efficiency, the articulation of the evils of politics upon administration, and the need to limit party influence in government.

Conclusion

From 1945 until the middle 1970s, the organization of the federal bureaucracy and civil service remained basically unchanged in terms of the ideology and values that structured it since the New Deal and World War II. Through the early 1960s the civil service was operating out of a New Deal and Progressive Era framework concerned with maintaining pyramid organizations and hierarchical lines of authority, and extending the merit and classification system to most of the federal government. Yet the 1960s Great Society and New Public Administration movements challenged that old order and questioned whether efficiency, rationality, and a technocratic or managerial ideology was the best model for the new social problems that federal bureaucracy confronted. Similarly, as it first became evident under Eisenhower, the success in implementing neutral competence ideology ran afoul of goals to use an administrative presidency to direct the bureaucracy in order to secure goals dictated by changing political imperatives.

On the one hand the New Public Administration movement suggested that administrators should be more client-focused and bureaucratic organization more open to employee and client participation through the decentralization and social diversification respecting, social equity and other non economic values in the operations and evaluation of its programs. On the other hand, politically neutralizing the bureaucracy meant less presidential control and with that, the federal bureaucracy acquired more of its own independent political power, which needed to be limited or otherwise constrained if it were to remain subject to checks by the president and Congress.

While the New Public Administration movement did have significant support and produced numerous changes, backlash to the Great Society, as well as Nixon's election in 1968, tempered many of its more ambitious plans. Thus, the 1960s appeared to have inaugurated a new public administration ideology, the era of "government by social workers," yet the Nixon-Ford years and eventually retrenchment of the Great Society during the Carter and Reagan years limited the depth of the reform this new ideology could have created.

Notes

1. Van Riper 1958: p. 441.

2. Malone & Rauch 1960: p. 762.

3. Van Riper 1958: p. 448; Malone & Rauch 1960: pp. 762-763.

4. *Watkins v. U.S.,* 354 U.S. 178 (1957).

5. *Barenblatt v. U.S.*, 360 U.S. 109 (1959).

6. For example, see: *Dennis v. U.S.,* 341 U.S. 494 (1951), among other cases where the Supreme Court upheld or otherwise permitted criminal penalties for engaging in communist activities.

7. Van Riper 1958: pp. 452, 455-460.

8. Van Riper 1958: p. 452-458.

9. Public Law 404, 60 Stat. 237-244, 1946.

10. Van Riper 1958: pp. 444, 490-492.

11. Brauer 1986: pp. 42-43.

12. Van Riper 1958: p. 487.

13. Somers 1954: pp. 131-151.

14. Van Riper 1958: p. 487.

15. Brauer 1986: pp. 8-11, 41; Hess 1976: pp. 62-65; Greenstein 1982.

16. Van Riper 1958: pp. 495-496; Mosher 1982: pp. 85-89.

17. Van Riper 1958: pp. 518; Arnold 1986: pp. 202-203.

18. Long 1949: pp. 257-264.

19. Mosher 1982: pp. 91-95.

20. Van Riper 1958: p. 499.

21. Levitan and Noden 1983: pp. 9-10.

22. Levitan and Noden 1983: p. 10.

23. Harrington 1962.

24. Hodgson 1978: p. 181.

25. Levitan and Taggart 1976: p 21.

26. Hodgson 1978: p. 245.

27. Moynihan 1969.

28. Bennis and Slater 1968.

29. Frederickson 1989: p. 97.

30. Waldo 1978; Frederickson 1975: pp. 161-167.

31. Ingraham and Rosenbloom 1989: pp. 118-119.

32. 397 U.S. 254 (1970).

33. Guy 1989: pp. 219-220. This entire issue of *PAR* is devoted to an assessment of the 1968 Minnowbrook Conference and the New Public Administration movement that grew out of it.

34. Lowi 1979; Lowi 1985.

35. McConnell 1966.

36. Niskanen 1971; Savis and Ginsburg 1973: pp. 70-85; Ostrom 1974.

37. Thompson 1979.

38. Brauer 1986: p. 150.

39. Nathan 1983.

40. Nathan 1983: pp. 55-56.

41. Aberbach and Rockman 1976: pp. 456-468; Cole and Caputo 1979: pp. 399-413.

42. 408 U.S. 593, 597 (1972).

Chapter VIII

The Carter Reform Years

Introduction: The Context of the Carter Presidency

The Carter administration came to Washington after Watergate when distrust of the government was high, and popular support of the office of the presidency low. America's recent failure in the Vietnam War added to an erosion of American pride and faith in government, including faith in a strong president. On top of all this, the oil embargo by the Organization of Petroleum Exporting Countries (OPEC) in 1973 and the resulting economic recession in this country added to a conservative backlash against government intervention domestically, and for a demand for government to scale back some of its more ambitious programs. These conditions, along with other international events, such as the Soviet invasion of Afghanistan, the second oil embargo by OPEC, the fall of the Shah of Iran and the taking of fifty-two American hostages all in 1979, would preoccupy and hamstring the Carter administration rendering it legislatively ineffective and with dwindling popular support by 1980.

Carter came to office with a distrust of the federal bureaucracy not unlike that shared by the American public and his Republican predecessors. While Carter remained committed to the maintenance of civil service laws and the merit principle, he shared a concern that the size of the federal bureaucracy had made it more difficult for the president to take control over it and govern. In addition, with congressional distrust of the presidency at a high point as a result of Watergate, the president's power over the bureaucracy seemed to be ebbing. The consensus between Congress and the president over how the federal service should be organized and who should control it seemed open for reexamination, and the Carter presidency and then the events in the 1980s allowed for reexamination of the structure of the bureaucracy.

CSRA-78

Perhaps the most notable innovation in the Carter years was passage of the Civil Service Reform Act of 1978 (CSRA-78). Like presidents before him who promised to reorganize a federal bureaucracy that appeared to be out of control, Carter came to office vowing to strengthen presidential control over the federal service and to create a senior management team to oversee the government's operations. In 1977, Carter commissioned a study group consisting of high level careerists and political appointees, directing them to develop civil service reforms. Relying on previous work dating back as far as the Hoover commissions during the Truman administration, the committee came up with the outlines of what became the CSRA-78.

The Act sought to give the president more control over the federal bureaucracy by creating a new set of career bureaucrats more policy-making than administrative. These individuals would be under more direct political control of the president so that he could better influence the operations of the federal bureaucracy. This reform altered both the politics/administration dichotomy and increased the power of the bureaucracy and civil service in light of decreased presidential power as a result of Watergate.

CSRA-78 increased the number of political appointees and widened the range of incentives employed to manage career bureaucrats. CSRA-78 introduced regular merit pay awards, particularly for high level civil servants. It also collapsed the old career supergrades, officials at the GS-16 to GS-18 levels, into a 7,000-strong six-rank Senior Executive Service (SES) with rank in "person" rather than rank in "position." The SES would have certain advantages over the previous designations, including increased ability to take sabbaticals and participate in career enhancement opportunities.

Other innovations of CSRA-78 include splitting the old Civil Service Commission into separate organs: the Merit Systems Protection Board (MSPB) to protect careerists from political reprisal, and the Office of Personnel Management to act as the government's basic personnel agency. The Act also codified collective bargaining and affirmative action regulations; created the Federal Labor Relations Authority (FLRA) to oversee labor relations programs; increased research on federal employment trends and the implementation of CSRA-78; increased protection for whistle blowers; and mandated that the Office of Personnel Management (OPM) develop a performance evaluation system for employees on which merit pay would be based.

While CSRA-78 had some real benefits for careerists, there were also some costs associated with the Act. Political appointees were given the power to transfer SES officials, at least after a 120-day waiting period at the start of a new administration. However, as the Reagan administration later demonstrated, there were ways to get around the waiting period through "voluntary" transfers.

The Act somewhat weakened the merit system by increasing the number of political appointees and by reserving some of the SES positions, up to ten percent overall and up to twenty-five percent in any one organization, for noncareer personnel. This provision had an important loophole: funded positions were not necessarily filled. In one federal organization, for example, both of the noncareer executive slots were filled while career SES were encouraged to transfer or retire until none of the eight funded career slots were occupied![1] This gave the president power to take over an agency.

While CSRA-78 was passed too late for Carter to take full advantage of it, it was widely praised by Reagan supporters and appointees.[2] Donald Devine, a former political science professor and Reagan's chief of the Office of Personnel Management, praised the Act as the crowning achievement of the Carter administration, and defended it in Jacksonian terms.[3] CSRA-78 was rather less popular among other students of public administration. Complaints tended to focus on the clear punishment-reward style of many of the Act's provisions.[4] Some criticized the bonus system as "...discouraging collaborative, organizationally oriented team behavior; instead it encourages individual aggrandizement at the expense of team behavior."[5]

Still others criticized the Reagan administration's use of the Act to augment its own power rather than strengthen general administration. Reagan appointees were particularly able to do this because of their own belief in "supply-side management" ideals focusing on individual incentives and measurable outputs rather than processes. This management technique enabled Reaganites to make full use of the Act's material incentives to mold subordinate behavior. Still, many who have studied their implementation agree that the reforms have had little impact, good or bad, save to have somewhat increased the power of political appointees. This was indeed one of the objectives of CSRA-78.

The Courts, Spoils, Affirmative Action, and the Federal Bureaucracy

Besides passage of CSRA-78, other factors profoundly influenced the organization of the federal service during the Carter years. Two involved a series of legal and court decisions that had repercussions through the Reagan administration and dealt with the issues of patronage and the representative quality of the federal bureaucracy.

In joining its opinions upholding the Hatch Act, in *Elrod v. Burns*[6] the Supreme Court struck a blow against the patronage system in Chicago and the surrounding Cook County. The Court ruled that a newly elected Democrat, Richard Elrod, could not simply fire Republicans on the basis of their party affiliation because such an action would interfere with the First Amendment free speech rights of those fired. To justify the use of party as a qualification for employment the government would have to meet the most rigid constitutional test that existed, a compelling state interest, to show that party affiliation served a legitimate governmental interest. Such a test is not easy to meet and this decision suggested that perhaps party affiliation was not always a proper qualification for employment and that for many positions, perhaps even higher level ones, local officials might not be able use a patronage reward system for their supporters.

The Court did try to limit its holding in *Elrod* to non-policy making positions, but drawing the line between policy and non-policy positions was difficult and some read the decision as having much broader application than the facts of the case suggested. While *Elrod* was a case involving local officials, it did leave open the question of its applicability to the federal government. Most importantly, because the decision was ambiguous, it was not clear whether or not party affiliation would be an unacceptable criterion of employment for the president to consider for senior policy-making officials or for appointments to his Cabinet, for example.

Four years later the Court produced a majority that appeared to clarify and answer many of the questions left over from *Elrod*. In *Branti v. Finkel*[7] the Court again reaffirmed its decision that party affiliation was not generally a permissible criterion for public employment. However, the Court went even further than *Elrod* and indicated that an employee did not have to show coercion into changing their party affiliation to keep her job. Employees could contest their dismissal if they demonstrated that the dismissal was merely for party membership or partisan reasons.

Additionally, the Court sought to clarify when party was a acceptable criterion of employment. It rejected the simple policy making versus administration distinction because it was not always an adequate dividing line. In some administrative positions party may be important while in some policy positions it may not. The Court laid down a rather vague rule that party membership could only be used for employment when a public agency demonstrated that "party affiliation is an appropriate requirement for the effective performance of the public office involved."

In both of these cases the Court ruled that patronage, at least its more overt use, was an unconstitutional violation of the First and Fourteenth Amendments (speech and association rights of employees.) Yet in both cases, but especially *Elrod*, the Court also provided other reasons chronicling the evil of spoils. For one, patronage damages the free functioning of the electoral process by stifling political belief and competing political activity. Two, in noting the history of the abuses of the spoils system, the Court argued that we had reached a national commitment to eradicate it from our political system and thus, the Court's decision was consistent with evolving standards of public administration. Three, patronage was inefficient, limited government effectiveness, and unnecessary to encourage accountability in the lower level civil service positions.

The Court, in both *Elrod* and *Branti*, as well as in subsequent decisions,[8] found little constitutional room for spoils and patronage within the federal bureaucracy. These opinions seemed to reinforce the 1973 decision in *United States Civil Service Commission v. National Association of Letter Carriers*[9] where the Court had ruled on the political activity restrictions found in the Hatch Act. The Court held that the national commitment to eradicating spoils and supporting the merit principle in government made the restrictions upon the political activity of federal employees a reasonable and legitimate interest of the government. In this decision, much like the above patronage cases, the Court recounted the history of the abuses of the spoils system and indicated that it was no longer an acceptable practice to modern conceptions of public administration.

The significance of these decisions was that the judiciary was willing to accept and perhaps even constitutionalize the politics-administration dichotomy, neutral competence, and the merit principle as rules governing the organization of the federal government. By practically constitutionalizing these principles, the Court reinforced older yet still important administrative principles. These decisions made it difficult for presidents (as well as state and local executives) to gain greater control over the bureaucracy by using party affiliation as a criterion for filling many if not most positions, and these opinions, especially the Hatch Act decisions, also made it difficult to force federal workers to become involved in the political activities of the ruling political party. Hence, the patronage and Hatch Act decisions ran at cross purposes to the objectives of CSRA-78, insulating the federal civil service even more than before from political manipulation by the president.

A second issue that became increasingly important during the Carter years was the issue of representation in the bureaucracy. As far back as the Jacksonian era there were demands for the bureaucracy to be more representative of the people it served. This debate over representative bureaucracy really took two forms. First was the issue of interest representation, i.e., members of the bureaucracy should adequately represent the views of its clients. A second type of representation is descriptive representation: the bureaucracy should socially represent or mirror the demographic background of the people it serves.

Calls for a representative bureaucracy took on new meaning during and after World War II and especially from the late 1960s on. During World War II, personnel shortages had increased the percentage of women and African-Americans in the federal government, but after the war the percentages decreased. During the war, President Roosevelt had issued Executive Order 11246, which required fair opportunity for African-Americans in private sector companies that had Defense Department contracts. In the late 1940s Truman ordered the integration of the armed forces and the disbanding of the old segregated African-American and white forces. However, neither of these orders was directed toward the federal service.

During the 1960s, as the civil rights movement gained momentum, New Public Administration advocates argued for a more socially diverse workplace to promote better client service and interest representation. As a result, several pieces of federal legislation placed limits upon discrimination in the federal government in order to encourage a more diversified or socially representative workplace. A 1974 amendment to an earlier age discrimination law made it illegal for the federal government to discriminate on the account of age against those who were forty to sixty-five. The 1972 Equal Employment Opportunity Act brought federal employers and government agencies under Title VII of the 1964 Civil Rights Act. This Act banned discrimination on the basis of race, color, religion, sex, and national origin and it also empowered the CSC to enforce employees' rights under this Act. It also mandated that each government agency develop special affirmative action plans to grant equal opportunity to all applicants. Other avenues to encourage equal opportunity included provisions in the 1866 Civil Rights Act[10] and Executive Orders 11478 and 11590, banning discrimination in executive agencies.

Throughout the 1970s the government sought to reconcile existing merit principles with the goals of affirmative action and diversity. While on the face it would not seem that a merit system would be discriminatory, that was not true. Through the 1970s the most popular way for the federal government to engage in merit hiring was to offer standardized tests for entry level positions. The PACE test (Professional, Administrative, and Clerical Exam) was the most frequently used exam and it covered over one-hundred entry level positions. In 1978, for example, over 135,000 individuals took the exam.

Studies indicated that while fifty-eight percent of all whites who took the exam passed, only twelve percent of African-Americans did.[11] PACE was challenged in court as discriminatory toward African-Americans and as a result of litigation in the late 1970s[12] the Carter administration agreed to abolish the test, find alternative hiring procedures, and fill vacant positions with African-Americans and Hispanics in proportion to the applicant population. The Reagan administration was not excited by this consent decree and initially contemplated a challenge to it, but did not and instead sought other means to comply with or circumvent the PACE rulings.[13]

Unions in the Federal Service

Throughout the Kennedy administration, unionization in the federal government was weak. Bans on strikes, limited collective bargaining rights, and their lack of formal recognition all placed barriers upon organizing. Kennedy's Executive Order 10988 in 1962 established the right of federal workers to organize, and Nixon's Executive Order in 1969 further established workers' and collective bargaining rights and created the Federal Labor Relations Council (FLRC) to mediate worker grievances. In the 1960s unionization increased, and by 1980, eighty-six percent of all blue collar and fifty-four percent of all white collar were organized representing 1.2 million workers or over sixty-one percent of the federal service.[14] As in the private sector, not all those covered by a union contract are members, with membership varying by workplace.

Four unions in the 1970s covered the vast majority of the positions unionized in the federal government. These included the largest one, the American Federation of Government Employees (AFGE, founded in 1932), and National Federation of Federal Employees (NFFE, founded in 1917), National Treasury Employees' Union (NTEU, founded in 1938), National Association of Government Employees (NAGE, founded in 1947). Numerous other private-sector-based unions, such as the International Association of Machinists (IAM) and the Service Employees International Union (SEIU) are represented in the government.

CSRA-78 brought changes that helped unions. It codified Kennedy and Nixon Executive Orders, granted legislative sanction to collective bargaining, and expanded the scope of issues that could be debated during negotiations, although it did not include salary or classification among of those issues. Instead, employee rights were the main issues granted bargaining status. The Act also replaced the FLRC with the Federal Labor Relations Authority (FLRA), an agency similar to the National Labor Relations Board, but with the authority given to a neutral arbiter and interpreter of federal management-labor and grievance disputes. While unions tried to use the FLRA to broaden collective bargaining issues, their efforts met with mixed success under Carter, and under Reagan they met with even less success as the administration placed unsympathetic individuals in the FLRA.

The federal unions are still weak when compared to those in the private sector. The FLRA and the government have consistently limited union rights, including the right to strike. Union rights have remained subordinate to the public interest or the needs of particular agencies, and Congress has generally been unwilling to relinquish its power to control salary and wage structures, thus leaving the unions in the position of having to lobby Congress (subject to Hatch Act restrictions) on these items.

Conclusion

The Carter years represented a transitional era in the organization of the federal civil service. On the one hand, Carter was clearly supportive of a professional bureaucracy emulating Weberian and Progressive Era organizational models. On the other hand, he also sought to reorganize the bureaucracy to gain greater presidential control over it. CSRA-78 reinforced the principles of both neutral competence and the politics-administration dichotomy while also seeking to enhance its accountability to presidential directives.

In addition to Carter inspired reforms, other forces pulled at the civil service during this era. There were attempts to diversify the workplace through affirmative action; unions gained enhanced political and bargaining power that somewhat compromised presidential control; and the courts placed limits upon patronage and upheld the Hatch Act and its limits upon the political activity of federal workers. Add to all this the general retrenchment of the Great Society that started under Nixon and the emerging negative attitude toward the government, government service, and Carter himself. What emerged was that by the start of the Reagan administration in 1981, the civil service was being pulled in many different directions as conflicting values and concepts of public administration were juggled and sought mutual accommodation.

Notes

1. Personal interview, January 9, 1988.

2. Huberty and Malone 1981; Devine 1985; Devine 1987; Sanera 1984.

3. Devine 1985.

4. Thayer 1978.

5. Huddleston 1987: p. 16.

6. 427 U.S. 347 (1976).

7. 445 U.S. 507 (1980).

8. *Rutan v. Republican Party of Illinois*, 497 U.S. 62 (1990).

9. *United States Civil Service Commission v. National Association of Letter Carriers,* 413 U.S. 548 (1972).

10. 42 U.S.C.A. § 1981.

11. Levitan and Noden 1983: pp. 111-113.

12. *Douglas v. Hampton*, 512 F2d 976 D.C. Circuit (1975); *Luevano v. Campbell*, 93 F.R.D. 68 (1981).

13. Levitan and Noden 1983: pp. 113-115.

14. Levitan and Noden 1983: pp. 7-8.

Chapter IX

The Civil Service Revolution
That Wasn't: The Reagan Years

Introduction

The Reagan presidency came at a time when many of the assumptions governing the federal service since the Progressive and New Deal eras were challenged. In seeking to bring about a conservative revolution to change the role of the federal government in American society, Reagan needed to increase his political control over the federal bureaucracy, and CSRA-78 aided in this cause. Moreover, Reagan's objectives necessitated challenging congressional control over the federal bureaucracy, and the 1980 shift in party control of the United States Senate enabled that challenge to occur.

Finally, the Reagan presidency inherited a federal government where numerous political forces contributed to a testing of recent methods of organizing the civil service. CSRA-78 held out the dual promise of further professionalizing the government by the creation of a politically neutral Senior Executive Service (SES), but this Act also enhanced presidential political control over the federal bureaucracy and thus reinjected politics and ideology into the management of the bureaucracy. Reagan's administration represented a playing out of these forces, as well as a rethinking of numerous other concepts of administrative organization and American politics. In the end, while Reagan did succeed in making several changes in the federal government, the changes were not an enduring legacy and by 1988, the Reagan civil service revolution had produced neither a smaller government nor necessarily a more accountable or manageable federal service.

The Anti-Washington Election of 1980

Reagan's landslide victory over Carter in 1980 was perceived by many to be a conservative triumph against Washington, big government, and the federal bureaucracy. Asking American voters "If they were better off now than four years ago," Reagan promised voters that he would increase defense spending, maintain social programs, cut taxes, and reduce the size of the federal government by returning power to the states and the people. In his rhetoric and campaigning Reagan had run a strong anti-government and anti-bureaucratic campaign which, once he became president, converted into programs claiming to cut red tape, unnecessary paperwork, and programs that were not efficient.

Reagan's anti-Washington campaign attacked Carter as weak, naive, ineffective, and unable or unwilling to act. The hostility of the Reagan attitude toward Carter, Carter appointees, and the federal service was so acute that it could not help but effect the change of power from one administration to another, and set the tempo for much of the Reagan attitude toward the federal government and civil service.

Given the pattern set by the last two Republicans to take office, it was probably inevitable that the Reagan administration would have troubled relations with career federal executives. These troubles were unquestionably enhanced by several factors. First, unlike recent predecessors, Reagan had won a big electoral victory, with seeming coattails that included the first Republican control of the U.S. Senate in decades. There was a perceived mandate due to the size of his victory, and the administration did all it could to capitalize on this perception.[1]

However, the 1980 election really did not reflect any sudden change in public opinion. Reagan and his top pollsters were well aware that they had no ideological mandate. Rather, a weariness with Carter, frustration that Iran was holding Americans hostage, strong Republican challengers who hoped to capitalize on both, and simple luck in senatorial elections (where the GOP pulled out most of the closer contests) produced the Reagan "mandate." For better or worse, those in Washington were slow to grasp these facts.[2]

Second, the new administration had a clear ideological agenda. Outside of Defense, the Reagan administration really wanted a lesser federal role wherever possible.[3] The Heritage Foundation publication, *Mandate for Leadership*, gave the administration a blueprint for change.[4] Notably, much of this blueprint was written by soon-to-be Reagan appointees, and Heritage attempted to serve as a personnel agency for the administration. As one Reagan appointee stated, "initially you had to be on the Heritage list to get a job." Later in the administration, Heritage efforts were much less pronounced, perhaps because few skilled people would want very-short-term positions.

Heritage Foundation members also served on policy transition teams set up to staff and outline policy for functional policy areas. These factors reveal that the Reagan transition was by far one of the most rapidly planned and effective in recent American history, with transition planning beginning more than six months before the election. Some of the transition planning was highly public. Other parts were not. For example, future White House personnel director Pendleton James spent the nine months before the election traveling around the nation talking to potential appointees, using his executive search business as a cover. He would periodically report to Edwin Meese at secret, early morning meetings at a Bob's Big Boy in Arlington.[5]

Third, the Reagan administration had a clear strategy for implementing its agenda. Learning from presidential agenda-setting from Kennedy to Carter, Reagan's legislative strategy led it to move fast while presidential popularity was still strong and before opposition could organize. Reagan officials used their capital wisely, focusing on economic policy and budgeting to the exclusion of nearly everything else in the early going. This fast movement and focus for executive energy helped the president win approval of the key provisions of his package.

The Reagan Appointment Strategy

The Reagan administration had a clear appointment strategy that was taken from the Nixon and Eisenhower years. First, political appointees were to be very carefully selected, and selection was to assure that officials met an ideological litmus test. As Henry Salvatori, a longtime member of Reagan's kitchen cabinet, remarked:

> The three main criteria we followed were, one, was he a Reagan man? Two, a Republican? And then, a conservative? Probably our most crucial concern was to ensure that conservative ideology was properly represented.[6]

A *National Journal* headline described the criteria simply: "Wanted: 275 Reagan Team Players; Empire Builders Need Not Apply."[7] Perhaps at its most extreme, Lyn Nofziger, an important official in the Reagan administration, remarked that "We have told members of the Cabinet we expect them to help us place people who are competent...As far as I'm concerned, anyone who supported Reagan is competent."[8]

The satisfaction of ideological and teamwork criteria was assured by instituting a series of checks on appointments, particularly relatively low level appointees who attracted little attention but often had considerable importance. Recent administrations had typically given Cabinet secretaries considerable leeway in building their own teams, often to the later chagrin of the White House. This was not attempted under Reagan. Instead, at the subcabinet level and sometimes even below, a series of senior Reagan officials including Ed Meese, James Baker, Michael Deever, Lyn Nofziger, Richard Allen, Martin Anderson, Fred Fielding, and the relevant Cabinet secretary each had veto power over an appointment.[9]

This review process became important when conservative activists charged that relative moderates such as James Baker had been dominating the appointments process in the first months of the administration, favoring relatively moderate "Nixon-Ford retreads." For example, Craig Paul Roberts, a staunchly conservative Reagan

Treasury official, typified the tensions when he lamented that "Presidents seldom know more than a few of their appointees and have no idea who they are relying on." He went on to recall his own swearing-in ceremony, at which the president urged his appointees to aggressively implement his agenda:

> A man sitting next to me asked if I was new to government. It was his third administration, he explained. All of a sudden the pleasure of breakfasting at the White House gave way to a sinking feeling that the Reagan revolution was running on retreads. I felt lonely and wondered if the President did.[10]

In March 1981, Nofziger pressed conservative demands within the White House, and the new appointments generally pleased the right.[11]

The extended appointment process, involving numerous interviews and separate clearances, took a long time and may have discouraged some individuals. Reagan EPA Head Ann Burford recalls her anger with the Byzantine process. Similarly, a low level appointee in one organization complained of the long, confusing appointments process which took several weeks:

> For the new person trying to get a job, it was a zoo. The Reagan transition was organized, but it was still a zoo. It was an organized zoo. I can't imagine a transition starting later! They wouldn't know who they appointed to what jobs...You could interview with someone one day, but would they have the same power the next day?[12]

Ideological criteria were not important only to the conservatives. Relative moderates were appointed to Cabinet positions. James Watt, Reagan's first Interior Secretary, was a notable exception. Generally, more politically extreme officials took lower level positions.[13] In part, this appointments process probably reflects the ideological divisions within the Reagan camp. The moderates dominated appointment in the first months when Cabinet level spots were filled. Their impact was to place experienced Washington hands in highly visible spots to promote Reagan policies in the press and Congress, while leaving more extreme officials in lower level positions to manage the bureaucracy. Here they would attract less controversy in the short term (save among their career subordinates), and quite possibly have great long term influence.

Impact of the Appointment Strategy

The involved appointment process and attention to relatively low level positions took time but also achieved the desired results. The Reagan appointees generally were conservative. Those in regulatory organizations, in particular, were quite likely to be from the businesses their new organizations regulated. Heritage Foundation officials had suggested that a careful appointment process could break up all subgovernments supporting big government.[14] Yet the Reagan administration seemed more intent on breaking up only some subgovernments, such as in social-welfare and regulatory agencies, so that it could control policy, while strengthening subgovernments in defense.

The Reagan administration appointed positions important to its overall agenda in OMB. The OMB would become an important political arm of Reagan that would police the bureaucracy.[15] The appointment strategy also placed key interest supporters (business) first while filling those important to minorities, consumers, workers, and union members only later or not at all. This put the latter groups at a disadvantage in the increasingly difficult budget fights.[16] Overall, Reagan generally placed technical and experienced experts in his favored organizations while selecting conservative ideologies for domestic agencies.[17]

Like Eisenhower, Reagan and his chief aides fully realized the need for teamwork among Cabinet members. Regular Cabinet meetings were used to indoctrinate officials. Cabinet councils, in contrast, were small groups of Cabinet and subcabinet members who met to work out functional policy decisions. These too, however, assisted in developing teamwork.[18] At the lower levels, the Heritage Foundation held a series of orientation sessions for new political appointees. These were designed to indoctrinate officials, introduce them to other political appointees, and teach them about their organizations before careerists could do it.[19]

When asked about these Heritage workshops, one political appointee stated that "the things they came up with were interesting, but naive. Most of it involves legislative change that won't happen." He also felt that the Heritage workshops urging appointees to distrust bureaucrats were impractical. Another official, a career SES member not generally sympathetic with the GOP, was invited to one of the Heritage forums by mistake:

> They were reminded that it was very easy to lose religion. One of the best ways to avoid this was to come to the monthly Heritage social gatherings. One of the _____ political appointees reported how he had improved the regional financial center in _____, improving the working conditions there. Someone turned on him and was just livid. She wanted to know why he wanted to improve conditions. Why not get rid of it? Contract it out? They were all after him then.[20]

Management of the Career Service

Reagan's ability to change the direction of the federal government resided in taking control of the federal bureaucracy and that required greater presidential control over department heads and the SES. While CSRA-78 was not available for President Carter to use to reorganize the federal service, Reagan employed it with much success.

Reaganites enthusiastically approved of CSRA-78 and used it to gain greater presidential control over the federal government by placing more conservatives in office.[21] Additionally, the Reagan administration used the 120-day no transfer clause as a manipulative tool during its early days by requesting certain Democratic members of the SES, or those heading up liberal social-welfare agencies, to agree to "voluntary" transfers as a way to get around the waiting period. One official in a domestic regulatory organization suggested that:

if one didn't cooperate, you didn't know where you'd end up.
Well before the 120-day limit: I "volunteered" for a transfer.
What a joke. They couldn't do it officially...They called you into
the __ floor, which is intimidating to start with, then they'd tell
you to sign your transfer.[22]

This experience contrasted sharply with official 1982 Government
Accounting Office (GAO) findings summarized in a report to
Representative Patricia Schroeder. The GAO report found no
involuntary transfers in the first 120 days of the administration and
few thereafter.[23] There were, however, hundreds of "voluntary"
transfers leading to a loss of morale and effectiveness among many
in the SES.

Some careerists indicated that noncareerists and appointees
used other means to take over organizations:

There's the mushroom theory, a brainchild that came out of
Heritage, you feed them [bureaucrats] shit and keep them in the
dark. The good old turkey farm: you can give someone no staff,
no responsibilities, and just leave them there, or you can leave
them in their current jobs, but bypass them. In EPA you could
have GS-12s with more power in the agency than the SESers.[24]

[They had] "the giggle factor," an arrogant review to decide
which R and D programs would continue and which would not.
The director and two [noncareer] assistants would look at it and
if all three giggled they'd cut the research.[25]

Generally, the Reagan administration succeeded in placing
more conservative political appointees into the federal government.
Yet statistics on the number of conservatives actually appointed are
misleading because professed conservative ideals may say little about
behavior. As one Heritage Foundation analyst suggested:

If you ask these guys, they know what to say. They're Attila the
Hun conservatives, but that may not say much about their
behavior. They know that they're supposed to be for free
markets, but what does that mean? So you find people like that
saying things like 'the market's fine, but people have to get a fair
price for what they produce.'[26]

Though most Reagan appointees were very conservative Republicans, they did not always agree among themselves. One self-described "Kennedy Democrat" and career SES member serving in the Office of the Secretary of Defense, maintained that ideological coherence did little to smooth over the usual sorts of conflict among Reagan appointees:

> ...there's been more trouble among the political appointees than between the political appointees and the civil service. You get an awful lot of knifing in the back, positioning for power, positioning for authority, positioning for policy victories. But that's just a small minority. Most don't have time for that crap...It has been a little worse in the Reagan Administration, a little more vicious. Some of the people in this Administration have followed and kept fighting after the people have left the building.[27]

If there was little agreement on the ideals among the Reagan appointees, there was also, not surprisingly, little agreement on the degree to which Reagan officials used the personnel system for blatantly political public administration. Certainly, as is noted above, Heritage writers on personnel management urged appointees to aggressively use the merit pay and transfer provisions of CSRA-78 to reward politically friendly SES and other high level careerists and punish or neutralize others. Within limits, such activities were legitimate, even intended by the Act.

Yet had such manipulation occurred? Few Heritage writers felt that CSRA-78 and other personnel levels were adequately or illegitimately employed, save possibly OPM Director Devine, who often defended the achievements of political administration under the Act. However, some did castigate Devine for his overly strong respect of the merit system:

> After Carter, this place was loaded with noncareer people converted to career. If that's the game, we should be able switch our people to balance the side. There is a mediocre attempt at best, and OPM has been highly uncooperative. The guy who worked under me, it took almost a year to convert him from noncareer to career. Finally, Senator _____ called Don Devine, and Devine said "I don't think so." He was philosophically

against it. _____ pressed, and it was done...[Later] they made an
effort to help noncareer switching, but they put a career person
in charge of it. They aren't doing a thing.[28]

Others disagreed. Former Civil Service Commission member
and American University Professor Bernard Rosen claimed that there
was an intense Reagan personnel effort and called the implementation
of CSRA-78 "a disaster for merit."[29] Rosen had been an original
opponent of the Act. But various public employee organizations
which originally supported or at least did not oppose the Act agreed
that Devine's OPM failed to protect careerists from political
reprisal.[30] Few regulations were written in that regard, and the general
thrust of Devine's administration, by his own admission, was to
increase efficiency and political responsiveness rather than protect
careerists from political manipulation.

According to some, Reagan management strategies, along
with the political use of CSRA-78, savaged the merit system,[31]
suggesting that "while the operation of the SES has remained, to date,
clearly within the bounds of the law, the provisions of the CSRA
have so expanded managerial prerogatives as to raise reasonable
doubts about the long-term stability of the balance between the
responsiveness and neutrality of the civil service."[32] A 1984 MSPB
report indicated that over fifty percent of SES members felt unprotected from arbitrary action, and over forty percent felt the system
was not free from improper political influence.[33] In general, the
impression civil servants had was that they were no longer as
protected or as safe as they used to be under previous administrations.

No matter the degree of political control of the career system,
the personnel cutbacks in the early Reagan years offended many
careerists. As early as Reagan's first inaugural speech he described
government as part of the problem and not as a solution and he
subsequently proposed a hiring freeze which became his first act as
president. In 1981 and 1982 the first large scale reductions in force
(RIF) were implemented under OPM guidance. Under the RIF
system, high level employees "RIFed" could bump lower level
employees into subordinate positions, taking their jobs while
retaining previous salary and benefits. Thus one RIF could often

affect three people. While only 11,000 RIFs were attempted government-wide, and 30,000 employees affected, these tended to be concentrated in certain activist domestic organizations, including the Environmental Protection Agency (EPA), Housing and Urban Development (HUD), and OPM itself.[34]

Predictably, morale and performance in effected organizations were greatly damaged, encouraging many individuals to leave voluntarily. Michael Sanera, then an assistant to OPM Director Devine, advised the OPM chief that RIFs tended to retard efficiency and outlined alternatives to effect cost savings. The Sanera memo on the matter was not distributed, and Devine allegedly wrote that it "should not see the light of day."[35] This suggests that efficiency in the many social-welfare and regulatory organizations was not greatly valued.

Overall, when examining employment in the federal service, in 1980 during the last year of the Carter administration there were 2,820,978 civilian workers in the Executive branch. By 1982 there were only 2,770,285 and it was not until 1984 that federal employment reached 1980 levels. When the last year of the Carter administration is used as a basis of comparison, only the Departments of Defense and State increased in employment while other departments and many regulatory agencies took cuts, some of which were severe.[36] By 1987, the majority of the staffing cuts occurred in a select group of agencies, with major personnel reductions in HUD, HHS, and the Department of Education approaching one-third of their personnel, while in Defense there was over a fourteen percent increase in staff.[37] Yet even these percentages do not tell the whole story. Within departments such as Justice, cuts were often concentrated in units such as the Anti-Trust Division, with particular missions of certain agencies significantly compromised.

Whether Reagan's actions led to an increase in the number of political appointees (at the expense of career civil servants) within the administration is also somewhat of an issue. Public administration writers often castigated the increased number of political appointees under Reagan. Certainly, in some organizations the numbers of noncareer executives increased significantly. Yet an overall increase is not clear. Best estimates indicated a slight increase of under five percent in the numbers of political appointees since 1978.[38] Most of this increase, however, came during the Carter Administration.

Perhaps more important were the "hidden appointees," known only to White House personnel-office staff. The feeling is that they have increased, though nobody knows for sure. Further, it is quite likely, though not demonstrated, that Reagan political appointees often served in positions higher than their ranks would suggest, while SES careerists were underplaced. Typically, Devine suggested that such slight increases as may have occurred mattered little, for "How one can be concerned with the 'pollution' of the career civil service when political appointees represent only .15% of all appointees is beyond comprehension."[39]

In sum, the Reagan appointment strategy, the use of CSRA-78, and the RIFs policy succeeded in giving the Administration greater ideological control over the bureaucracy by placing conservative and supportive appointees and SES members at the head of most of the important federal agencies. Yet the appointment strategy, in the long run, did little to decrease the size of the federal government or the percentage of workers covered by civil service laws.

Reagan and Labor Unions

Federal labor unions were given more political and bargaining power under Title VII of CSRA-78. Despite this power and a mixed reception and record under the Carter administration,[40] their success under Reagan was limited and relations between them and the president were poor.

During Reagan's first year he was able to use the appointment process of CSRA-78 successfully to gain greater partisan control over both the Merit System Protection Board and the Federal Labor Relations Agency (FLRA). In the case of the latter, the president effectively ignored holdover Carter appointees and replaced its general counsel with one more sympathetic to his agenda. As noted earlier, the FLRA was created to replace the Federal Labor Relations

Council (FLRC), precursor to the FLRA and created in 1969, and remove from it and individual agencies the authority to resolve labor grievances. The FLRA and the MSPB were meant to be neutral agencies, yet their partisan control by the administration questioned their impartiality throughout the Reagan years.[41]

The first and most dramatic confrontation between Reagan, FLRA, and the federal unions occurred in 1981 during the first year in office. The federal air controllers union, PATCO, representing about 15,000 employees, was engaged in negotiations with the federal government over numerous issues, with the most important being reducing the work week and improving the working conditions for the controllers at many of the busiest airports.[42] While PATCO had started negotiations under Carter to resolve grievances, under Reagan an impasse in negotiation had occurred. Partly the impasse could be attributed to PATCO's determination to acquire private sector bargaining rights, or perhaps its plans and preparation for a strike, but the administration also undertook three actions that forced a break-down of negotiations in the summer 1981.

In February, 1981, the administration hired a Washington, D.C. law firm with a reputation as a "union-buster" to undertake negotiations with PATCO. Then Reagan appointed J. Lynn Helms to head the FAA. He also had a union-busting reputation. After that, the FAA had prepared and updated a Carter strike contingency plan that would have permitted more flights per day than had the Carter plan. This change in number of permitted flights would have considerably weakened the PATCO strike that many feared would have shut down the U.S. airports.[43]

After both PATCO and the FAA had failed to agree to a new contract, PATCO went out on strike on August 3, 1981. This strike clearly violated the Taft-Hartley provisions that made strikes by federal employees illegal. Four hours after the strike began, Reagan stated that any striking controller who did not return to work within forty-eight hours would be fired. Approximately 5,000 never went on strike or returned, thus leaving 11,301 controllers out of work. Subsequently, the FAA moved to have the FLRA decertify or withdraw union recognition from PATCO, which it did, and the decision was eventually upheld in federal court.[44]

The PATCO firing and decertification was clearly the most severe test of federal union and presidential power in American history, and it could also be described as the lowest point in such relations. Clearly PATCO engaged in an illegal strike, yet the Reagan administration's bargaining strategy and appointment of union-busters suggest that it may have been forcing a strike. The PATCO incident, while not again repeated in the Reagan administration, did set the tone for eight years of unfriendly federal union relations. Under Reagan, workers received smaller raises than in previous years and they lost several important cases including mandatory drug testing under certain conditions.[45]

Reagan Management and Personnel Practices

Beyond what has been described as the president's political administration of the bureaucracy, there were several other important actions undertaken by Reagan to control the government and reorganize the civil service. First, Reagan made as his highest priority the elimination of waste, abuse, and fraud in the federal government. To secure that goal several techniques were used: the Office of Management and Budget (OMB) became a political arm of the president. Second, under David Stockman, his first OMB director, the agency was empowered to review the regulations of other agencies and limit unnecessary paperwork or ensure that the regulations proposed were cost effective.

In the first case, the Paperwork Reduction Act of 1980 was used to limit regulations, while in the other, a Reagan Executive Order mandating that a cost-benefit analysis be performed on proposed rules was required and used to prevent agencies from promulgating new regulations. OMB's use of both review mechanisms was instrumental in redirecting agencies and personnel to adopt goals more sympathetic to the administration, in reducing social-welfare and regulatory power, and in moving the government away from many of the equity-orientated goals and concerns of the New

Public Administration reforms.

In 1981, a second attack on waste and fraud occurred when Reagan created the President's Private Sector Survey on Cost Control (PPSSCC), otherwise known as the Grace Commission, to review the personnel and organizational practices of the federal government and to make recommendations for ways to eliminate duplication, unnecessary procedures, waste, etc. The Commission was funded privately, and it produced forty-seven reports that included 12,000 pages, thirty-eight volumes, and almost 2,500 recommendations for reform and potential savings.[46]

These recommendations urged that the government adopt many private sector business techniques, including changes in military procurement policies, use of paralegals instead of lawyers in some departments, and the closing of many small post offices and branch Social Security offices.[47] Many of the Grace Commission recommendations were adopted, and Reagan repeatedly asked Congress to adopt the rest, but many of the proposals were criticized as changing the very goals of government rather than increasing efficiency.

Third, as noted above, partisan and nonpartisan use of RIFs in the first Reagan administration somewhat decreased the size of the federal government. However, from 1984 on, the size of the federal civilian employment increased steadily, surpassing the Carter administration levels and topping out at 3,090,699 in 1988 at the end of the Reagan administration.[48] This was the largest civilian employment level since the end of World War II. Increases in employment did not occur uniformly, but were concentrated in the Defense, State, and Justice Departments as well as the Veterans Administration, with cuts still occurring in many domestic and regulatory agencies.

Fourth, while perhaps not a reformer, Reagan came to office as a strong opponent of the affirmative action and personnel diversification programs the Justice Department, the CSC, MSPB, and the EEOC had created. He opposed the goals and timetables that the federal government had been using to encourage more employment of women and minorities, and often the Justice Department was required to oppose measures that would give them preferential treatment. Moreover, the Reagan administration had originally planned to contest the consent decree that Carter had negotiated to resolve the PACE lawsuits, yet it opted not to and instead instituted new decentralized noncompetitive hiring procedures for entry level positions.[49]

Despite this action, there is some evidence that white male employment dropped from fifty percent to forty-one percent from 1976 to 1986. By 1986, men and women divided about 50/50 in the federal workforce. By 1986, approximately sixteen percent of the workforce was African-American with another nine percent comprised of other minorities.[50] Overall, the Reagan bureaucracy continued to diversify, but most of the minority and female employment remained at lower levels. Senior positions tended to fall to older white males who were usually compensated much better than most women and minorities.

Finally, after the early use of CSRA-78 to move around SES members, and the appointment of many conservatives, the initial careerist and presidential appointee conflict between administration and agency goals was resolved in the second term in one of three ways. In those agencies such as Defense there never was a conflict and thus no accommodation needed to occur. In some agencies no accommodation ever occurred and the Reagan appointees never trusted careerists. Careerists left and were replaced by appointees. These changes could be taken as a sign that the Reagan capture of the bureaucracy was successful, at least in some areas, or that accommodation of administration and bureaucratic goals had occurred in some areas.

Conclusion

The Reagan presidency raised numerous questions about the management of the federal bureaucracy and the civil service. It placed into direct conflict demands for presidential political control of the bureaucracy and demands for the civil service to be a politically neutral administrative organization somewhat resilient to the political imperatives of the chief executive. The Reagan administrative policy of using RIFs, cutting back or demoralizing SES members in some agencies, and using ideological appointments increased, at least in the short term, presidential control over the federal bureaucracy, thus demonstrating what CSRA-78 could do if properly manipulated. Reagan's administrative policy in his first term created significant conflict between careerists and noncareerists who differed on the policy and mission of selected agencies.

Did the Reagan revolution cause a revolution in the management of the civil service? The answer to this question in part depends on whom you speak to or upon your political preferences. It did demonstrate to a significant extent the political power of the president as the head of the federal government, and in the process questioned the desirability of the bureaucracy as a politically independent check upon the chief executive. On the other hand, those who disliked the political direction of Reagan see his eight years as an example of how inexperienced appointees can disrupt the efficiency and goals of an organization by alienating it from its clients.

The Reagan revolution did question and perhaps move the federal government further away from the Great Society and New Public Administration reforms by reasserting traditional hierarchial commands of authority. His actions did not represent a total abandonment of the ideology of "government by social workers" and its replacement with spoils as a major public administration ideology. Yet the former was weakened and the latter was reinvigorated to a degree.

But what the Reagan Revolution never really did was successfully attack the politics/administration dichotomy or reverse the overall trend of covering more federal positions by civil service laws. Although the Reagan administration sought greater political control over the federal service, it sought to achieve that not by disbanding with the merit system or by repealing the Hatch Act. Instead, it reinforced the politics/administration dichotomy by seeking to increase management control in a way that would allow greater policy control at the top with the bureaucracy faithfully executing delegated policies. The Reagan administrative agenda sought to neutralize bureaucratic power by placing it under presidential control, yet by 1988 it was unclear how successful they had been.

In addition, in 1990, two Supreme Court decisions struck blows against presidential political administration of the bureaucracy. First in a 7-2 decision, the Court ruled in *Dole v. United Steelworkers of America*[51] that provisions of the 1980 Paperwork Reduction Act that the Reagan OMB had used to police the regulatory and rule-making authority of other federal agencies was illegal. This ruling in effect threw out one of the more important tools that the Reagan era had created to take policy control over from the bureaucracy. Second and more importantly, in a 5-4 decision, the Supreme Court extended its earlier rulings in *Elrod v. Burns* and *Branti v. Finkel* and held in *Rutan v. Republican Party of Illinois*[52] that "promotions, transfers, and recalls after layoffs based on political affiliation or support are impermissible infringement on the First Amendment rights of public employees." In stating that to "the victor belongs only those spoils that may be constitutionally obtained," Justice Brennan and the majority defended the political neutrality of the bureaucracy and reinforced the constitutional ban upon the use of patronage in most personnel decisions. Both decisions reinforced protection of the civil service against politics and political manipulation by the president and other outside forces.

Hence, by the end of the Reagan era, it was unclear either how much he had changed the organization of the federal service or how much power the president had taken back from Congress, the courts, or the bureaucracy.

Notes

1. Brauer 1986: pp. 220-221.

2. Jacobson 1983; Pomper 1981; Ranney 1981.

3. Nathan 1983; Newland 1983: pp. 1-21.

4. Heatherly 1981.

5. Walker and Reopel 1986: pp. 734, 739-742; Brauer 1986: pp. 223-228.

6. Bonafede 1981a: p. 609.

7. Kirschten 1980.

8. Newland 1983: p. 3.

9. Similar review processes and ideological tests were also conducted in the Justice Department for potential appointments to the federal judiciary.

10. Roberts 1984: p. 125.

11. Kirschten 1981; Bonafede 1981b: p. 3.

12. Maranto 1993.

13. Nathan 1983: pp. 12, 69; Bonafede 1987: pp. 48-49.

14. Huberty and Malone 1981: pp. 869-901.

15. Newland 1983: pp. 11-12.

16. Nathan 1983: pp. 75-76; Newland 1983: p. 3.

17. Newland 1983: p.4.

18. Nathan 1983: pp. 72-73.

19. Nathan 1983: p. 75.

20. Maranto 1993.

21. Mackenzie 1987.

22. Maranto 1993.

23. GAO 1982.

24. Maranto 1993.

25. Maranto 1993.

26. Maranto 1993.

27. Maranto 1993.

28. Maranto 1993.

29. Newland 1983: p. 15.

30. Newland 1983: p. 18.

31. Kirschten 1983; Ingraham 1987a; and Huddleston 1987.

32. Huddleston: p.7.

33. Ingraham 1987b: p. 431.

34. Kirschten 1983: p. 735; Rubin: 1985.

35. Brownstein 1983: pp. 711-712.

36. Department of Commerce 1987: p. 311.

37. *Ibid.* p. 318.

38. Ingraham 1987: pp. 427-430.

39. Knott and Miller 1987: p. 248.

40. Masters 1985: pp. 612, 622-623.

41. Northrup and Thornton 1985: pp. 16-21.

42. Hurd and Kriesky 1986: p. 115.

43. Hurd and Kriesky 1986: pp. 120-121.

44. Northrup and Thornton 1985: pp. 27, 99.

45. *Skinner v. Railway Labor Executives Association*, 489 U.S. 602 (1989); *National Treasury Employees Union v. Von Raab,* 489 U.S. 656 (1989).

46. Goodsell 1984: p. 198.

47. Goodsell 1984: p. 199.

48. Department of Commerce 1989: p. 321.

49. Ban and Ingraham 1988: p. 708.

50. Lewis 1988: p. 701.

51. *Dole v. United Steelworkers of America*, 494 U.S. 26 (1990).

52. *Rutan v. Republican Party of Illinois*, 497 U.S. 62 (1990).

Chapter X

Government Service as a Noble Calling: Bush and the Civil Service

President Bush and the Return of Neutral Competence

Coming of age during World War II and the Cold War in a time when foreign policy was largely bipartisan, President Bush felt at home with a centrist bureaucracy. While leading the Central Intelligence Agency (CIA) in the Ford administration, George Bush insisted that the CIA not have a single position, but rather present various intelligence estimates to the president so he could decide. Such staff work is in the best traditions of a politically-neutral career bureaucrat. Indeed, in the 1977 presidential transition CIA Director Bush urged President Carter to reappoint him to ensure a nonpartisan intelligence policy. Similarly, in his inaugural address President Bush urged Democrats in Congress to remember the time of their parents when "politics stopped at the water's edge."[1] Such centrist patriotism seemingly appealed to career federal executives, most of whom reported having voted for George Bush in the 1988 presidential election.[2]

The Bush civil service seemed a much kinder and gentler place than Reagan's and represented a return to the values of public administration that sustained a politically-neutral career civil service over the last one-hundred years. As the first president to succeed a member of his party since 1928, and the first sitting vice-president to be elected president since 1836, the Bush administration had a relatively peaceful transition and rather good relations with the career civil service. The new president had no mandate for change, and indeed, seemed to lack an ideological agenda, much to the disappointment of many conservative activists.[3]

Prior to his election, President Bush had lived in Washington for most of the previous twenty-two years, and he seemed to understand and empathize with the career bureaucracy.[4] He did not attack the Washington bureaucracy. He took time in the first months of his administration to speak at a Senior Executive Service luncheon to praise the talent and dedication of the federal careerists. In sharp contrast to his predecessor, Bush declared that "Government service is a noble calling and a public trust." Indeed, this appearance was recalled fondly by SES members four years later:[5]

> President Bush called us over individually, as many of us as he could, to say that the fate of the government depended on the SES. It was really a magical experience. I think Bush was very honest about that. I believe at the time he meant it, and it put us a year or two ahead of the usual transition.
>
> [The Clinton transition] is not unlike the Reagan transition, but it's a fairly significant contrast with Bush. Bush had a real conception of what a career civil service is all about. His first appearance [as president] was before the SES! He also took pains to praise individual careerists he met on presidential fishing trips and the like.

Overall, George Bush was probably the most openly pro-civil service president since Herbert Hoover and his actions toward the civil service have done much to repair the poor relations that festered under Reagan.

Centrism and support for neutral competence were reflected in President Bush's appointment criteria, which differed notably from President Reagan's. While President Reagan represented a conservative movement and stressed ideological change, President Bush wanted appointees who would be good stewards of their agencies.[6] In place of ideology, the Bush White House emphasized loyalty, competence, ethics, and diversity, in roughly that order. Moreover, Bush's appointees reflected his relative support for ethical purity and expertise in government rather than for conservative mandates.[7] Early in 1989 Bush called for a tightening of ethical disclosure acts and standards in response to the HUD, the Iran-Contra Affair, and other publicly-disclosed abuses in the Reagan administration.

A Bush White House Personnel Office official boasted that "we had very few crooks, very few wife-beaters. The President simply did not accept unethical behavior." In the Departments of Housing and Urban Development and Health and Human Services, career civil servants considered Bush appointees more ethical than their Reagan predecessors, yet there were few differences in the rest of government.[8] Regarding diversity, the Bush White House Personnel Office recorded the demographics of appointees and pressured top appointees to consider ethnic, gender, and geographic diversity in fashioning their teams. This was done quietly and on a piecemeal basis, without quotas. In contrast, later on, the Clinton White House would insist on approving whole slates of officials at a time to assure diversity.[9]

Career executives recognized the changes from Bush to Reagan. In a 1993-94 survey of 613 career federal executives, SES, and GM-15 levels serving in the Washington offices of twenty federal agencies,[10] substantial majorities or pluralities of careerists saw Bush political appointees in their agencies as more competent, more moderate, more ethical, and more trusting and supportive of career bureaucrats than Reagan appointees. Career bureaucrats also thought Bush appointees relatively less likely to support the White House and more likely to support the agency or department, thus validating the observations that the Bush administration featured less of the White House orientation of the Reagan administration and something more akin to cabinet government.[11]

Ethics and reporting requirements combined with President Bush's appointment criteria slowed the pace of subcabinet and Schedule C political appointments. In addition, an unexciting Bush agenda, relatively low pay levels for government executives, and the increased scrutiny given government executives, e.g., the rejection of John Tower as Secretary of Defense, led many prospective appointees to refuse positions. The problems were particularly severe in a

Defense Department already facing downsizing, mission changes, and the implementation of the Goldwater-Nichols Defense Reform Act. Twenty-four people approached about the position of Undersecretary of Defense for Acquisitions turned it down. Pentagon career executives lamented that:

> We used to have captains of industry and CEOs, now we get staff from the Hill, assistant professors, associate professors, staff from think tanks and universities. One of the reasons is the revolving door law. Donald Atwood only came in because he was going to retire. Guys like that come in knowing they can't go back to the private sector.[12]

Few careerists from domestic agencies voiced similar concerns, probably since the most qualified non-Defense appointees come from state and local governments, academe, small businesses, and congressional staffs rather than from industry.

An unusual number of the top Bush appointees, including four Cabinet secretaries, were longtime personal friends of the president. A GAO study found that twenty percent of the Bush appointees felt that the president had personally arranged their appointments; forty-nine percent felt that other political appointees had arranged the appointment and nineteen percent listed Congress.[13] The 1992 GAO survey of Bush Senate-approved appointees found that almost sixty percent lived in the Washington area before their appointment.[14]

Yet there was far less attention to normal party patronage than usual. Indeed, much to the annoyance of party professionals, most administrative jobs in the 1990 census were filled through civil service procedures rather than traditional patronage.[15] The Carter and Reagan administrations appointed many Georgians and Californians who did not like Washington, though some decided to stay there. In contrast, the Bush appointees were far more likely to have considerable Washington experience. Real estate agents mourned that thirteen of the sixteen Bush cabinet secretaries and perhaps half the subcabinet appointees were already Washington residents.[16]

Though these individuals were Washington residents and Republicans, they were not necessarily Reaganites. As one GOP insider remarked, "A premium is put on Bush loyalty" and "that's why Reagan people are having to leave."[17] One Bush supporter who served in both Republican administrations noted the value of having an FBBI button ("For Bush Before Iowa"), referring to those who supported George Bush even before the 1980 Iowa caucus briefly made him the frontrunner for the GOP nomination. Most of those who had FBBI buttons got jobs in the Reagan Administration, and found upward mobility in the Bush years. Conservatives criticized the Bush administration for neglecting ideological policy reforms,[18] and the forced exodus of Reagan followers from the executive branch following the 1988 election left hard feelings. As one Heritage Foundation analyst remarked in 1993:

> The Bush people had no ideology, and they were stupid. They came in and laid off all the Reagan people. Now the ex-Reagan appointees are all over K Street and the Bush appointees are asking them for jobs. As you can well imagine, the reception is less than warm and friendly.

Indeed, surveys suggest that only seventy percent of Bush appointees were Republicans, eighteen percent Democrats, and six percent independents.[19] A survey of Reagan appointees found one percent Democrats, seven percent independents, and ninety percent Republicans.[20]

Bush personnel first estimated that only about ten percent of the Reagan appointees would continue to serve under President Bush. In fact, as of summer, 1989, about thirty-five percent of the Bush subcabinet appointees had served in the Reagan administration, though not always in the same jobs. In part this reflected the difficulty of finding new appointees who were both competent and willing and able to withstand increasingly difficult ethical checks and FBI background investigations mandated in the wake of Watergate and the later financial scandals of the Reagan years. It was often easier to leave subcabinet officials in place rather than find qualified successors.[21]

Unlike the Reagan administration, which had a well-defined executive strategy, the Bush administration did not employ careful ideological litmus tests on new appointees.[22] Bush gave Cabinet secretaries considerable power to select their own teams. This, and the president's unwillingness to use the White House to ride herd over the Cabinet led some to call the Bush Cabinet the most powerful since Eisenhower's. Bush, one of the few recent presidents who did not talk about Cabinet government, may have been the one closest to implementing it.[23] Indeed, while the Reagan administration placed larger numbers of political appointees in central management agencies, the Bush administration did not target specific agencies since it used political appointees less to manage government and more to reward supporters.[24]

Since there was no pressing need to alter a federal establishment whose top layers were managed by Republicans for the previous two terms, the pace of presidential appointments was exceedingly slow. Aside from loyalty, President Bush sought to appoint technically-competent, ethically-correct, diverse individuals. This may have allowed OMB managers to dominate the policy agenda in the first year of the administration, but it also offended some career executives who wanted clear directives to follow and were anxious to meet their new bosses.

Still, the relative moderation of the administration and its willingness to allow presumably subgovernment-oriented Cabinet secretaries to choose their own teams suggested an administration far more in tune with Washington norms, and far less likely to have attempted to reorient the missions of federal organizations in ways antithetical to careerists serving within those organizations. Perhaps the great stock of experienced Republicans available for high level service after years of GOP rule over the executive branch dramatically lessened the tensions between political leadership and careerist-neutral competence, in at least three ways.

First, their experience in government had lessened the antipathy of conservative Republican activists to the career civil service, who, they have found, actually tend to follow the dictates of their bosses when possible. Second, by the end of Bush's term the career civil service had served under Republican chief executives for twenty of the previous twenty-four years. William Kristol, Vice

President Quayle's chief domestic policy adviser and the former chief of staff to Education Secretary William Bennett, noted that the long GOP domination of political appointee levels is "bound to have an effect, at least because of the kinds of things they'll have been asked to think about." At Education, Kristol recalled finding "more receptivity to Reaganite and Bennett-like ideas than I had expected."[25]

Finally, it was suggested that career bureaucrats are influenced by the promotion policies of their political bosses, and even more by the intellectual debates of American society as a whole, which over the last fifteen years have been increasingly conservative.[26]

Personnel Issues under the Bush Administration

Given the relative peace between the Bush Administration and the permanent government, it is not surprising that the story of the Bush civil service focussed on technical personnel issues rather than dramatic challenges to either political control or career expertise. Bush chose Constance Newman to be his Office of Personnel Management (OPM) chief. She was a management consultant who had worked her way up from a GS-3 clerk-typist to a HUD undersecretary and VISTA director during the Nixon-Ford years. Newman was also the first African-American to hold the post. Bush allowed Newman to decide her own agenda, and she attempted reforms of pay and performance appraisal systems.

For example, the administration proposed "locality pay," a concept first advanced by Nixon. This would pay those at the same grade level more if they lived and worked in high cost cities. For years, the civil service had difficulty attracting employees to high cost cities, and could seldom get high level careerists in field offices to accept promotions to Washington jobs whose pay increases would barely match the increased cost of living. Organizations adapted by placing those doing comparable work in higher civil service grades if they worked in high cost areas, but these efforts were neither systematic nor always sufficient.

Locality pay gained lukewarm support from some federal

unions, and geography worked against the proposal since there were more congressmen from low cost than high cost areas. Further, some feared that such proposals could actually work to decrease the aggregate payroll. Yet locality pay passed Congress in 1991, and it allowed for additional awards of up to eight percent of base pay in such high cost cities as San Francisco, New York, and Washington. Figuring out the exact amount of the locality pay awards, which are not always funded by Congress, was a serious issue for civil service unions.

Newman also publicized the problems of attracting and holding competent secretaries, clerks, and other support staff. While the spread of word processors through the white collar ranks decreased support staff, somewhat lessening the urgency of the problem, there were still demands to recruit well-qualified people and encourage them to pursue a career in the public service.[27]

Yet in high cost cities such as Washington, in particular, Newman maintained that the government had too many offices in which there are a "few people who work and others who wander around and fuss. Managers say, 'If I tighten up, I'll lose them.' The way some phones are answered, it might be better to let them ring."[28] To address these personnel problems, Newman offered a combination of higher pay, easier procedures to terminate employment, retraining of employees, and working with local school systems to attack adult illiteracy. She also proposed increasingly systematic merit pay provisions, eliminating automatic step increases with seniority rather than for performance.

The long term payoffs of Newman's efforts remain unclear. Notably, at both blue collar and white collar ranks, there continue to be far more applicants for federal positions than there are positions to fill. Perhaps this suggests that relatively flexible working conditions, good benefits, and employment security continued to make federal work attractive. In addition, virtually all SES members were recertified, and the SES won a twenty-two percent pay raise. This decreased the numbers of SES members moving to the private sector.

Finally, on the upper end of the civil service, in 1989 Director Newman successfully introduced proposals to substantially increase the pay of SES members, while at the same time enabling top officials to "recertify" the executives every three years. Seemingly, this would both stem the flight of experienced federal managers to the private sector and somewhat enhance the control of political appointees over careerists. The change was supported by the Senior Executives Association.

Of course, not all the activity affecting the civil service was the result of administration efforts. Other initiatives also had a long term effect upon federal personnel. First, in 1989, the National Commission on the Public Service, headed by former Federal Reserve Chairman Paul Volker and former Cabinet Secretary Elliot Richardson, addressed many of the problems that Newman noted and proposed numerous recommendations to revitalize the federal service. Among these recommendations, they advocated dramatically decreasing the numbers of political appointees from 3,000 to 2,000 and increasing the numbers of careerists serving at the highest levels of government. To a great degree, their arguments reflected disenchantment with the perceived ideological fervor and frequent scandals of political appointees in the Reagan years. But their arguments also indicated that excessive numbers of political appointees do not increase political control and instead compromise efficient and competent administration and the development of a career civil service.[29]

Moreover, this Commission proposed numerous reforms to diversify the civil service by increasing women and minorities in the bureaucracy. Other recommendations were to increase worker productivity, augment technical support for specific bureaucracies and agencies, and develop new pay and personnel performance standards. While Bush endorsed many of these proposals, except those related to reducing political positions, the status of the recommendations of the Commission may or may not have had the same impact that similar recommendations of the Hoover Commissions had forty years earlier. Many of these recommendations, particularly those regarding increased technical support and pay flexibility, were to be echoed and acted upon in the course of the Clinton administration's Reinventing Government reforms.

Second, during the Carter and Reagan administrations, the federal government increasingly contracted out federal services. The Bush administration continued this trend, but civil service organizations and public administration academics were generally skeptical of contracting out. Opponents argued that contracting out was a threat to the long term integrity of the civil service, had not been shown effective, was ripe for scandal, and weakened the power of the federal managers to provide quality service since it removed them from the day to day operation of government programs. Proponents argued that contracting out increased the flexibility of government service while decreasing the cost. For better or worse, it seems likely that there will be no consensus on contracting out in the near future and small experiments, including privatizing the Postal Service in such communities as Binghamton, New York in 1990, will continue.[30] Both the Bush and Clinton administrations have increased the use of contracting out, to the point that some critics complain that the federal government is becoming a "hollow state" without adequate capacity to either provide services or monitor those who do."[31]

Third, attacks on the Hatch Act materialized in 1990. In 1990 a radical revision of the Act which would have allowed federal employees to seek party offices and solicit party funds at their workplaces only narrowly failed to survive a presidential veto. Low level employees' unions have long favored repeal since it could increase their political clout. Democrats in Congress generally favored repeal because of their belief that most federal employees are Democrats. Government executives, on the other hand, have generally opposed changing the original Act since it could lead to pressures to work for the party in power. Apparently agreeing with this assessment, President Bush justified his veto with concerns about the neutrality of the career service,[32] and by one vote in the Senate his veto was sustained.

Conclusion

President Bush supported civil service traditions of technically competent, politically neutral public service. The president praised the civil service, increased its pay, respected its expert advice, and by and large appointed competent, ethical officials who shared his respect for the permanent government. President Bush began the deregulation of pay systems which paved the way for President Clinton's reinvention of government. Yet Bush's non-partisan management style failed to bring coherence to the executive branch, and was perhaps not in keeping with the more ideological tone of modern American politics.[33] Still, were it not for the ill-timed 1991-92 recession (the economy improved just too late to help the Bush reelection effort), the Bush style might well have proved more successful than the more partisan Reagan presidency. In any event, the Bush administration was certainly kinder and gentler to the career civil service than his predecessor's.

Notes

1. Pfiffner 1990; Maranto & Schultz 1991; Rockman 1991.

2. Maranto 1994.

3. Germond and Witcover 1989.

4. Pfiffner 1990.

5. Maranto 1993: p. 16.

6. Weko 1995; Pfiffner 1990.

7. Solomon 1989.

8. GAO 1992.

9. Maranto 1993.

10. Maranto 1995.

11. Maranto 1994; Maranto 1996.

12. Mackenzie 1989.

13. GAO 1992.

14. Michaels 1995: p. 276.

15. Devroy 1989.

16. *National Journal* 1989.

17. Solomon 1989: p. 1057.

18. Podhoretz 1993.

19. Michaels 276.

20. Maranto 1993: 101.

21. Pfiffner 1990: pp. 67-69.

22. Solomon 1989: pp. 1057-1058.

23. Pfiffner 1990: p. 67.

24. Ingraham 1995.

25. Barnes 1989.

26. Barnes 1989: p. 278.

27. Haveman 1989a; Haveman 1990b.

28. Haveman 1989.

29. Haveman 1989.

30. Kane 1990.

31. Milward 1994.

32. Dowd 1990.

33. Maranto 1993.

Chapter XI

The Clinton Administration
and the Future Civil Service

*We cannot put people first and create jobs and economic growth
without a revolution in government...We can no longer afford to
pay more for—and get less from—our government. The answer
for every problem cannot always be another program or more
money. It is time to radically change the way government
operates — to shift from top-down bureaucracy to entrepreneurial government that empowers citizens and communities to
change our country from the bottom up.[1]*

Introduction

Clinton management of the executive branch can be thought
of in two parts. In defining its priorities and staffing executive branch
political appointments, the Clinton administration got off to a slow,
disorganized start. In part this reflected the President's own decisions
and decision style. But there were also deeper causes: a less consensual Washington culture and the fraying of the presidential appointment and Senate confirmation system due to partisan differences.

In sharp contrast, the Clinton management of the career civil
service is perhaps the most innovative since the heady days of the
New Deal. In many respects President Clinton will be known as a
president of achievement, deepening or broadening regulatory reform,
partnerships with the states, and most importantly, the whole tangle
of "reinventing government" reforms from Vice President Al Gore's
National Performance Review (NPR). In 1992 candidate Clinton
promised policies "neither liberal nor conservative, neither Democratic nor Republican."[2] At least regarding government administration, most of the Clinton policies are in fact neither liberal nor
conservative, but instead focus on the delivery of government

programs rather than their content. Accordingly, most of the Clinton/Gore initiatives have the potential to stand the test of time and change the direction of the federal service. Indeed, most of the Clinton administrative reforms accord with an international movement toward results-based management ("Does it work?") rather than process-based management ("Does it follow regulations?"). Despite the likelihood of significant long-term success, at least in matters of public administration, the Clinton administration did not have an auspicious start, and throughout the Clinton presidency numerous factors contributed to Clinton's inability to secure many of his political and policy goals: his lack of political mandate; partisan conflict with Congress, including change in party control of both the House and the Senate; and public demands to change the federal government.

A Centrist Election
in a Conservative Era

Until the summer of 1992, most Washington observers thought President Bush likely to win reelection. Bush failed in his quest chiefly for four reasons. First and most important, the economy was in recession. President Bush's advisers mistakenly expected a recovery before the election, and the Bush administration never developed and sold to the public a plausible response to the recession. Second, Arkansas Governor Clinton waged a masterful campaign organized around three themes: economic renewal, "change versus more of the same," and the need for universal access to health care. In contrast, the Bush campaign was slow to react to Democratic charges and lacked a coherent theme. Third, Ross Perot's maverick third party campaign drew votes from the Republicans, and in any event stressed the need for change. Finally, in contrast to previous Democratic nominees and to much of the party's (mainly northern) congressional leadership, the southern Bill Clinton ran as a centrist, pro-business New Democrat rather than a traditional "tax and spend" liberal Democrat. This was exemplified by various Clinton stands, including support for the death penalty, a middle class tax cut, free trade, "reinventing" the federal bureaucracy, and cutting 100,000 civil service positions. In a three-way race Governor Clinton won only forty-three percent of the popular vote, the first president to win with less than a majority since 1968. Despite taking the White House, the Democratic party failed to gain any seats in the U.S. Senate and actually lost ten in the House of Representatives, perhaps because large majorities of Americans saw deficit reduction as a high priority and wanted, at least in theory, to cut both taxes and the size of government.[3] In practice, many voters wanted tax cuts, benefit increases, and deficit reduction even though these goals may be impossible to reconcile.

"Hitting the Ground Walking": Clinton Policy and Appointments

Once elected, President Clinton faced the tasks confronting all new presidents, i.e., choosing priorities and staffing his administration. On both counts, President Clinton got off to a slow start, "hitting the ground walking." President Clinton's reluctance to come to closure on such administration initiatives as the economic program and health care reform played a role in scuttling parts of the former and all of the latter.[4]

Much of the slow pace of President Clinton's appointments occurred because of factors beyond the president's control. A long absence from the White House left the Democratic party with little institutional memory about how to staff the executive branch. This overwhelmed the Clinton transition, with great numbers of Democratic job applicants desperate to take advantage of a chance to serve their party and country. More important, like all recent presidents, President Clinton centralized appointments in the White House rather than allowing cabinet secretaries to choose their own teams, mainly to assure White House control over policy and representation.[5]

In addition, increasingly cumbersome and complex FBI investigations and financial disclosure rules made it more difficult to select would-be officials than in the past. Since the passage of the 1978 Ethics in Government Act, political appointees have been required to list their financial assets, which could then be obtained by reporters through a Freedom of Information Act (FOIA) request. Officials could also be told to place certain assets in blind or semi-blind trusts. To keep a campaign promise, President Clinton strengthened existing restrictions by insisting that appointees agree not to lobby their own agencies or for foreign governments for a period of five years after leaving government.[6] Such restrictions have had particularly severe impacts on areas requiring appointees with substantial business experience, as in defense procurement. Surveying the landscape, one long-time Pentagon bureaucrat lamented in a 1993 interview, "each new administration adds to [ethics rules] on the assumption that we're a nation of crooks." Another complained that "we used to get captains of industry and CEOs. Now we get staff from [Capitol] Hill, assistant professors..."[7]

Other factors also compromised the appointment process. These factors included a more divided elite community in Washington, increased interest groups and public comment on appointments, and perhaps a more polarized and less polite nation.[8] For example, more contentious congressional hearings managed by congressional staffers and interest groups seeking to deny confirmation to the other party's nominees made it more difficult to find and confirm well-qualified nominees. In addition, talk radio and other new media gave the nomination process a more populist and public tone, especially in contrast to the Reagan confirmation process in 1981. While the vast majority of presidential appointees at the assistant secretary level and above (requiring Senate confirmation) were approved with little fanfare, a few attracted great controversy. For example, a scandal erupted with the disclosure that Attorney General designate Zoe Baird had hired illegal aliens for baby-sitting and other tasks.[9] Though Baird's actions were legal at the time, the specter of a millionaire lawyer hiring illegal immigrants for child care enraged public opinion and stopped her nomination. Other nominees were blocked on ideological grounds, as when Clinton's choice to direct the Civil Rights Division of the Department of Justice, Lani Guinier, was (perhaps unfairly) labeled a "quota queen" for her academic writings. White House Counsel Vincent Foster, a longtime friend of the president's, complained in his suicide note that in Washington "ruining people is considered sport." Of course one could point to Robert Bork, John Tower, and other nominees of Republican presidents who met similar fates at the hands of Democratic congressional staffers and interest groups.[10] As a result of increased controversy, increasingly lengthy FBI background checks, and complex ethics requirements, the average length of time needed for selection and confirmation has steadily increased over time, going from approximately two and one-half months under President Kennedy to over four and one-half months under Carter to eight months under Bush and eight and one-half months under Clinton.[11]

Yet President Clinton also bears some of the blame for the slow pace of appointments. Like most candidates for president, Clinton failed to initiate adequate transition planning during the election, so as not to seem overconfident. After the election, the president-elect ran the transition from Little Rock rather than Washington in order to emphasize his commitment to changing the status quo. For much the same reason, at least in domestic policy areas, the new administration tended to shut out those with experience in the Carter administration. The process of appointment was also flawed. During the transition period the president-elect selected his transition personnel chief, former South Carolina Governor Richard Riley, as Secretary of Education. The president-elect waited a month before replacing Riley, delaying the appointment process. Insufficient staff resources were allocated to personnel functions, in part to satisfy a campaign promise to cut the White House staff. The process was further delayed because Bill Clinton, Hillary Rodham Clinton, and certain of her associates all took an active role in the appointments process, making it difficult to come to closure on decisions. In particular, Bill Clinton sought to appoint a diverse administration which "looks like America" regarding ethnic, gender, and geographic diversity. As a result, instead of offering nominees one at a time, Clinton proposed slates of appointments to ensure that the slate had the appropriate gender, ethnic, and geographic balance. Proposing such slates, though, slowed down the appointment process in comparison to the more traditional means of appointment used by previous presidents.

Clinton appointees were fifteen percent African-American, six percent Hispanic, and forty-six percent female, all impressive given the small pool of potential applicants owing to past discrimination. For the first time, a few openly homosexual citizens were appointed to subcabinet positions, signaling increased public acceptance of homosexuality and enraging influential Republican North Carolina Senator Jesse Helms and anti-gay groups. At the same time, moderate and conservative Democrats may have been underrepresented in key positions, thus weakening Clinton's ties to the party regulars.[12]

Finally, President Clinton was unable to make rapid appointments in part because of his decision-making style, and in part because of his past experience in Arkansas. The Arkansas governorship had few political appointees, and in the small state the governor personally knew all the likely contenders for jobs.

Hence, given the party's long absence from the White House, it was inevitable that any Democrat elected president in 1992 would have had comparable problems staffing the executive branch. Indeed in some respects complaints about the tardy Clinton transition can be likened to those of President Wilson in 1913 and President Eisenhower in 1953, whose parties also spent many years without controlling the executive branch.

The slow pace of appointments and the controversies faced by many Clinton appointees led to soul-searching among academics and Washington insiders. Yale law professor Stephen Carter argued in his 1994 *The Confirmation Mess* for a shorter, more polite nomination process focusing on objective qualifications and philosophical views rather than attacks on nominees' lifestyles and academic writings. The Twentieth Century Fund issued a report in 1996 suggesting, among other things, that the numbers of appointees be reduced, that FBI investigations of prospective appointees be modified and in some cases eliminated, that conflict of interest laws be simplified and post-government employment restrictions eliminated, that the Senate should "fast-track" more confirmation hearings, and that civility be restored to the process.[13] Whether these or other reforms will be adopted remains to be seen. Yet given the concern for government corruption and interparty competition, the latter enhanced by the party change in Congress in 1994, it does not appear likely that these reforms will be adopted soon.

The Clinton Administration and Career Executives

Perhaps in part because in 1992 candidate Clinton stressed domestic policy themes and because many Washington elites saw President Bush as out of touch with the nation's needs,[14] survey data revealed that Bill Clinton won the votes of most high level (GM-15 and SES) career bureaucrats serving in Washington, doing particularly well among those serving in the generally liberal, activist social-welfare and regulatory agencies.[15] Only Defense Department bureaucrats, who are relatively conservative, backed Bush. In contrast, data from the same sample suggest that Bush won the 1988 vote among career government executives.

Despite the problems facing appointees, interviews and surveys in the first eighteen months of the administration suggested that in most domestic agencies President Clinton's appointees respected and were respected by the career bureaucrats serving under them. Indeed career-noncareer relations were comparable to, and in social welfare and regulatory agencies, even better than during the bureaucrat-friendly Bush administration. These good relations seemed to reflect ideological congruence. The liberal or moderately liberal Clinton appointees were more like the domestic career bureaucracy than were their more conservative Bush or (especially) Reagan predecessors. In the relatively conservative Pentagon, however, there were some tensions between career executives and Clinton political appointees. The military had even less trust for the Clinton White House, which was thought of as anti-defense. In particular, the Pentagon was troubled by budget cuts, a relatively activist and inconsistent Clinton foreign policy in Bosnia and elsewhere, and the president's proposal to allow openly homosexual citizens to serve in the military.[16] The latter personnel policy, issued early in the Clinton administration, was subsequently opposed by both Republicans and Democrats in Congress, resulting in the adoption of the "Don't Ask, Don't Tell" policy that effectively overturned the Clinton proposal. This policy precluded homosexuals from declaring their sexual orientation but it also banned the military from inquiring into the sexual orientation of military personnel.

Even in domestic agencies, certain Clinton policies troubled federal career executives. Determined to cut the number of federal employees to the lowest total since the Kennedy administration in time for the 1996 election, the administration employed the first non-defense reductions-in-force since the Reagan first term.[17] Unlike the Bush administration, the Clinton administration made few efforts to raise federal pay. The administration also empowered unions at the expense of federal managers, and may in a few instances have moved to isolate federal executives who were not supported by their agency unions. The administration's emphasis on ethnic and gender diversity in political appointments and promotions within the career civil service offended some white male employees, but also heartened many women and minorities and could be justified by the traditional glass ceiling in the career service.

Finally, the president's signature of Hatch Act modifications making it legal for the civil service to become involved in political campaigns threatened the politics-administration dichotomy compromise in effect since the New Deal. But repeal of some Hatch Act provisions also enabled civil servants to enjoy the full rights of citizenship in a democracy. The Act's provisions prohibiting political activity at the office and outlawing political coercion remain in place. No significant abuses of the new system have yet been reported. In the 1996 congressional elections, public sector unions helped defeat a number of Republican Congress members, but the GOP still retained control of each House of Congress (even gaining seats in the Senate) despite President Clinton's easy reelection. Whether the union election activity will earn public sector workers more respect (and perhaps higher pay) from politicians, or simply provoke the

Republican Congress to seek revenge, is not clear.[18]

Bureaucracy's End?: The Reinventing Government Paradigm

> *Too many of our public systems just don't work, and money alone won't fix them. Think about it. Is there anything more foolish than spending more money for something that doesn't work? —Vice-President Al Gore*[19]

Perhaps the highlight of President Clinton's New Democratic agenda was the National Performance Review led by Vice President Al Gore. In some respects the NPR has its intellectual origins in two decades of conservative and neoliberal critiques of government bureaucracies that had been around since the 1970s. Politically, the perceived government failures of the 1960s, including Vietnam and the Great Society programs, led many neoliberal Democrats to conclude that Americans would never support an activist government until convinced that government could work. Neoliberal critics such as Charles Peters, editor of the *Washington Monthly* and mentor to a number of influential journalists, increasingly joined traditional conservative critics of bureaucracy in arguing that all too many government programs were inefficient, strangled by red tape, and opposed to such basic American values as discipline and patriotism. Unlike Republican conservatives, many of whom wanted to dismantle federal government programs, most neoliberals wanted to reform government so that it could again play a positive, appreciated role in civic life.[20] Such views were found throughout the Clinton/Gore 1992 campaign book, *Putting People First*, which promised to cut 100,000 federal positions and to reform a number of government programs in order to discourage irresponsible behavior and reward those who work hard and play by the rules.

Fiscal crises also drove the reinventing government movement. On the state and local level in the 1980s and 1990s, social problems such as crime and continued public demands for more services collided with increased opposition to higher taxes. This tension pressed innovative managers to find new and better ways either to provide services more efficiently, or else focus on key services and end the public provision of others.[21] On the national level, the same dynamic was pushed by deficit spending. Rising entitlement spending and public opposition to tax increases drove the deficit in the 1980s and 1990s, pushing politicians and bureaucrats alike to seek new efficiencies without actually cutting benefits to voters.

The need for cost savings was clear. Moreover, a plethora of business and public administration writings argued that the government could in fact be made more efficient through new management doctrines stressing deregulation of the civil service, less hierarchical or "flattened" management, and by having government bureaucracies compete with other government organizations and those in the private sector. In the business world, such works as Charles Peters's *How Washington Really Works*[22] and Charles Peters and Robert Waterman's *In Search of Excellence*[23] argued that greater efficiency and innovation were achieved by freeing employees to do their jobs, encouraging innovation, rewarding success, and cutting layers of middle management and red tape that interfered with the actual work. To attain successful innovation, companies had to accept and not punish failure, encourage constant learning, and focus on customer service and basic missions. Flatter, more fluid companies focused on achieving their missions.

Some critics of bureaucracies sought to make companies less hierarchical and more democratic. In a somewhat more traditional vein, the 1993 best-selling *Reengineering the Corporation* argued that companies could make dramatic gains by "reengineering" business processes. Reengineering meant redesigning work processes by training employees to do various jobs. This reduced the division of labor in order to encourage innovation and end bottlenecks and transition costs in the production process. Often it involved innovative uses of information technology, which allowed one employee to do a greater number of more sophisticated tasks. In effect, the "reengineering" claims updated Taylor's classic scientific management theory. Like Taylorism, reengineering is fundamentally a top-down reform of work, though it may empower lower level workers by giving them less routine jobs.

However, the bible of the federal effort to reinvent government was the 1992 *Reinventing Government*, by journalist David Osborne and consultant and former city manager Ted Gaebler. The authors argued that the fall of communism and the seeming incapacity of traditional government bureaucracies to solve basic social problems had delegitimized the hierarchical, bureaucratic, civil service paradigm adopted by the Progressives. To ascertain what should come next, the authors explored more than a dozen state, local, and federal government success stories in search of lessons for innovators. While readable, optimistic, and insightful, *Reinventing Government* was not without flaws. It is repetitive, occasionally contradictory, and cliche-ridden (e.g., "Steer, don't row"), and some of its success stories may reflect good public relations rather than good management.[24] Still, the journalistic work of Osborne and Gaebler combined with more scholarly treatments by others to present a coherent new paradigm in government management.[25] Chiefly, the Reinventing Government paradigm endorsed several principles.

First, competition and free markets innovate rapidly and provide services efficiently, but government is still needed to solve collective problems and assure justice and social equity. Yet by using market structures and mechanics, public administration can take on some of the favorable attributes of markets. Second, government services need not always be provided by government bureaucracies. Instead, a variety of alternative arrangements can be employed. Examples include: contracting out; giving vouchers to individuals which enable citizens to choose their own services; awarding franchises which governments grant or sell to service providers (as is now done in most government site restaurants); and stimulating competition in which units of government compete with either the private sector or with other government agencies. For example, magnet schools are public schools which compete with both public and private schools for students.[26]

Third, when government provides services, it can do so more

efficiently and effectively by changing government culture and organization structure in a number of ways. These changes include cutting red tape by eliminating rules and simplifying or eliminating paperwork. In particular, complex procurement and civil service personnel systems designed to prevent wrongdoing were perceived to have become so cumbersome that they also prevent innovation. They make it too difficult to hire, fire, and retain government employees, and keep the government from buying what it needs when it needs it.

Other innovations also included cutting middle management and headquarters; changing organization structure by having fewer hierarchical relationships and more teams bringing together those with different specializations; using multi-year lump sum budgets rather than line budgets to give bureaucrats more discretion about how to spend their money; emphasizing variety in service provision, rather than "one-size-fits-all" public monopolies; and using information technology, focusing on measurable results, holding bureaucrats accountable by using financial rewards and punishments, and changing organizational culture to emphasize innovation, customer service, and actual results rather than compliance to regulations.

In short, the Reinventing Government paradigm argued for letting a thousand flowers bloom, with the notion that at least a few will blossom into beautiful roses. Though borrowing from some of the Reagan era reformers, the Reinventing Government paradigm did not disparage public workers. Rather, it saw federal workers as good people trapped in bad, bureaucratic systems. It was this mantra which guided the vice president's National Performance Review (NPR).

Reinventing Government

After six months of intensive effort by nearly two-hundred officials, nearly all of them career civil servants, along with Reinventing Government teams in every department and major agency, in 1993 Vice President Gore presented the National Performance Review to President Clinton in the White House Rose Garden.[27] Its almost four-hundred major recommendations paralleled many of the Reinventing Government themes, including calling for changes in personal and organizational policies, budgeting, and the use of technologies. It also called for the increased use of contracting out, forming partnerships with unions to improve quality, the adoption of customer service standards, and the implementation of the Government Performance and Results Act of 1993 (GPRA) which mandated that agencies formulate strategic plans with short and long range goals and measures of success.

In short, the National Performance Review was a bold declaration of the Reinventing paradigm, with specific recommendations. Unlike Reagan's Grace Commission, and all too many private management schemes, the NPR was actually formulated by career civil servants, people who knew the system and had first-hand knowledge of its flaws.[28]

Knowing that the ultimate success of reinventing depends on culture change, the vice president toured federal workplaces around the nation to promote the NPR, even doing guest spots on "Late Night With David Letterman" to announce that no longer would the General Services Administration (GSA) issue nine pages of specifications for purchasing "ash receivers, tobacco (desk type)," i.e., ashtrays. He also used a forklift to dump hundreds of pounds of personnel regulations which OPM would no longer force agencies to follow.[29]

Many federal managers supported the Reinventing Government paradigm. A 1994 survey conducted between three and six months after the NPR report found that a plurality of career federal executives serving in Washington agreed that the NPR would "improve the operation of my agency." This was a high level of support given that the NPR proposed cutting back the number of officials, particularly executives in headquarters operations in Washington. Only in the Pentagon did a plurality oppose Gore's recommendations.[30] Anecdotal evidence and a few case studies suggest that many federal line managers felt frustrated by restrictive personnel, budget, and procurement rules. Of course, personnel, budget, and procurement specialists did not necessarily agree with this assessment.[31]

Perhaps most typically, agencies selected which parts of the

NPR they wanted to adopt and how and when to adopt them. This strategy fit into the NPR's emphasis on values and culture rather than rules and laws. In some cases agencies had taken existing ideas, such as a customer service initiative in the IRS, and sold them as NPR related in order to cement the support of the Clinton administration.[32] This does not suggest the weakness of the Reinventing paradigm, but rather that it has origins apart from any single political administration, and is thus likely here to stay.

In essence, the NPR is part of a broader social movement in public and private management rather than a mere administrative initiative. The decentralization of the NPR has led to a number of fascinating innovations, some of which demonstrate that its success does in fact depend on long term culture change. For example, the Office of Personnel Management (OPM) no longer mandates use of the hated SF-171, the standard government employment form which could take several days to fill out. Instead, one can now apply for federal employment using a simple resume. While many agencies have made this change, a few still use the SF-171 simply because they are used to it. Still others have designed new procedures nearly as obtuse as the old! In general, however, the NPR goes along with a long term trend toward using contractors and officials outside the official merit system (such as Schedule B employees, who sign limited term contracts which are normally renewed), simply because the merit system is seen by some as cumbersome.[33]

Some of the most interesting innovations have occurred in the use of market incentives. Increasingly the GSA (procurer of government ashtrays) has to compete with private firms for contracts serving federal agencies, and this has improved customer service. Many support agencies now operate under "revolving funds," meaning that they do not receive direct appropriations from Congress, but rather must convince other agencies to pay for their services. For example the Federal Executive Institute is a training facility operated by the Office of Personnel Management. It is a profit-making government bureau funded by charging other local, state, federal, and even foreign government agencies for services. Such an organization focuses much more on customer service than one dependent on congressional appropriations would.

Interesting regulatory reforms are also being undertaken as a part of the Reinventing Government movement. The Clinton administration expanded previous reform efforts into the EPA Common Sense Initiative (CSI). CSI has a number of components, including allowing regulators to suspend certain regulations for polluters who are meeting required emission reductions. CSI also brings polluters, regulators, and environmentalists together to share information about how to employ innovation technologies to pollute less, while not increasing regulatory costs. It thus encourages innovation and focuses on results rather than processes. CSI and related programs follow the models of public administration proposed by Reinventing Government advocates.

In short, the civil service is changing rapidly, and it is possible that the federal civil service of 2007 will be much more fluid and flexible than the current version.

Prospects for Permanent Change

Despite the many positives, the NPR can only be evaluated over the long term, and its ultimate success is by no means assured. The NPR proposed cutting back the federal bureaucracy by 252,000, and saving $108 billion over five years. Congress has enacted much of the legislative components of the NPR, and follow-up reports suggest that such savings may in fact be attained.[34] Yet from both the administration and Congress, many of the NPR cuts are "numbers driven" rather than based on careful analysis. Privatizing government functions may have long-term costs, including a loosened ethical climate and inattention to infrastructure. It may not be realistic to expect agencies to become more entrepreneurial at the same time that they are downsizing and individual workers are either looking elsewhere or fighting to retain their jobs. This is particularly true since managing relations with other organizations and private contractors requires substantial expertise, and NPR-related downsizing may cause skilled personnel to leave for the private sector.[35]

The NPR is in great measure about culture change, and even if over several years the culture of the bureaucracy is altered, this would not affect the culture of Congress. Congress has not approved all of the NPR ideas, particularly those regarding budgets and changing the personnel classification system.[36] In part, this opposition should not be surprising because many of the NPR reforms would weaken congressional control and oversight of the federal bureaucracy, strengthening the executive branch at the expense of the Congress.

More important, it seems likely that some of the empowerment given bureaucrats will be taken away once those same bureaucrats begin to make mistakes, or act in ways that Congress or political appointees disapprove of. If that occurs, one could see a return to Progressive-style bureaucracies, and new regulation writing to undo the NPR reforms.[37] Even without congressional re-regulation of the civil service, threat of lawsuits from interest groups or disgruntled employees unhappy with policy or personnel decisions provides powerful incentives for federal managers to be less than bold and innovative.[38] Further, if the government is reinvented but the public remains dissatisfied with government, perhaps because of unrealistic expectations of what democracy can deliver, then reinventing government will represent a hollow victory.[39]

Future Challenges Facing the Federal Civil Service

Regardless of how successful President Clinton's reforms are, change is never permanent in American politics. Numerous challenges and pressures will continue to affect the structure, values, and organization of the federal civil service regardless of who is president and what the composition of Congress looks like after the 1998, 2000, and subsequent elections.

As stressed throughout this book, the politics of civil service reform is influenced by numerous conflicting goals. These goals include using the bureaucracy as a source of presidential political patronage; employing the bureaucracy to promote neutral and efficient administration; permitting the president to have increased political control over the bureaucracy; and situating bureaucratic power within the larger domains of Madisonian democracy that enable congressional and judicial oversight and limits on bureaucratic and executive power. Whatever the merits of any particular reform proposed by Clinton or a future chief executive, fears of increased presidential power or institutional jealousy among the major branches of the national government will prompt new reforms or measures to limit or augment the political power of Congress, the courts, or the president. In addition, while at present public and partisan pressures are devolving power away from the federal government, future domestic or foreign crises will no doubt necessitate an increased demand for national action, thus demanding new regulations, personnel, and policies to address these new needs.

Much in the same way that the New Deal, World War II, and the rise of trusts during the Progressive era produced demands for new governmental structures, future social changes will similarly require new federal action. Additionally, while the development of spoils during the Jacksonian era was viewed initially as a reform, only later to be condemned as corrupt, present day reforms may soon be viewed as dated, corrupt, or inefficient, necessitating change. Hence, because society changes, and because of the multiple demands for the federal government and bureaucracy to serve different goals, the federal service will continue to face pressures for change.

But beyond any pressures that have confronted the federal bureaucracy since 1787, there clearly are some other challenges that the federal service faces in the near future. First, there will be continued pressure to diversify the workforce so that it reflects the changing demographics of an increasingly multicultural America. In the past the federal government has led the way, employing women and African-Americans at a time when no one else would,[40] and it seems certain that despite the backlash against affirmative action in some quarters, there will continue to be pressure for the federal government to maintain employment policies that encourage diversification.

Second, at least in the short term, a divided government unable to agree on the basic goals of the federal government is certain to influence the structure of the civil service. Republican congressional efforts to return some national power to the states or to limit the scope of the welfare state will continue to weaken the bureaucracy. At the same time, apparent bipartisan agreement to balance the federal budget by the year 2002 will threaten the size of the federal bureaucracy and at the same time increase the pressure to make the existing federal agencies and organizations more efficient. Hence, while the former will certainly weaken the bureaucracy, the latter may enhance the discretion and power of the president and federal managers.

Third, the federal courts cannot be discounted in the role they will continue to play in supervising the operations of the regulatory state. It is unlikely that federal judges will abandon completely their oversight of federal personnel and regulatory policies. For example, in 1996, the Supreme Court for the fourth time stated that the use of party affiliation or political views cannot be considered when hiring and firing public workers.[41] In the 1996 cases, the Court extended its previous rulings to apply to independent contractors. Thus, the Court seems determined to limit patronage as a tool of employment, at least below the policy-making level.

Finally, current attitudes toward the federal government will no doubt change as the Baby Boomers continues to age and a new generation of citizens comes of age. With that transition, new demands on the federal government will materialize, threatening current political alignments and any uneasy consensus there is regarding what the federal government should do or how it should operate. What this final factor attests to is that both in the short and perhaps in the long run, the changing fortunes of politics will continue to influence what the federal government should do, how it should be organized, who shall be hired, and who shall have control over the federal bureaucracy and civil service.

Notes

1. Clinton and Gore 1992: pp. 23-24.

2. Clinton and Gore 1992: p. viii.

3. Abramson 1995; M. Nelson 1993; Podhoretz 1993.

4. Pfiffner 1996: pp. 148, 176-81.

5. Weko 1995.

6. Mackenzie and Shogan 1996; Pfiffner 1996.

7. Maranto 1993a: pp. 12, 13.

8. Ginsberg and Shefter 1990; Uslaner 1993.

9. Nor was child care the only family-related issue dogging the selection of appointees. Given that most middle and upper class women now have full-time careers other than homemaker, it was often difficult for the Clinton administration to convince prospective appointees to come to Washington without also providing employment for spouses, who would otherwise face either separation or career interruption. In some cases the administration responded by finding political appointments for the spouses of appointees. Solomon 1993c.

10. Carter 1994; Mackenzie and Shogan 1996; Pfiffner 1996.

11. Pfiffner 1996: p. 169.

12. Carter 1994; Maranto 1993a; Pfiffner 1996; Solomon 1993; Weko 1995: p. 102. In some cases the emphasis on diversity led to ironies, as when Agriculture Secretary Mike Espy, the first African-American to hold the post, had his initial slate of underlings blocked by the White House for insufficient diversity. Maranto 1993a: p. 33.

13. Mackenzie and Shogan 1996.

14. Dionne 1991.

15. Maranto 1994.

16. Maranto 1993; Maranto 1995.

17. Notably, the vast majority of the Clinton administration's planned cutbacks were from attrition, from positions funded but not filled by actual people, or else were long-planned Defense Department cutbacks made possible by the end of the Cold War; thus the actual pain inflicted on the bureaucracy and the disruption to public service was less than many supposed. Maranto 1993.

18. Barr 1996; Barr 1997; Maranto 1993; MSPB 1996.

19. Barr 1993b.

20. Peters and Nelson 1978; Peters 1992; Marshall and Schram 1993; Howard 1994.

21. Barzelay and Armajani 1992; Osborne and Gaebler 1992; Marshall and Schram 1993.

22. Peters 1989.

23. Peters and Waterman 1982.

24. Maranto 1993.

25. Savas 1987; Barzelay and Armajani 1992; Garvey 1993; Durant 1992; Horner 1993; Kelman 1990; and Hult and Walcott 1990.

26. There are numerous other examples. Osborne and Gaebler 1992: pp. 332-48, list thirty-six separate means of service provision, though many are some variation of these four.

27. Gore 1993; Gore 1994.

28. Gugliotta 1996.

29. Gore 1993: p. 27; Gore 1994; Shoop 1993.

30. Maranto 1994.

31. Horner 1993; Maranto 1993; Ban 1995.

32. Maranto 1993.

33. Ingraham 1995; Kettl 1996.

34. Gore 1995: p. 7.

35. Goodsell 1994; Kettl and DiIulio 1995; Maranto 1993; Shoop 1993; Williams 1990.

36. Kettl 1996.

37. Meacham 1993.

38. Garvey 1993.

39. Hibbing and Theiss-Morse 1995.

40. Aron 1989; King 1995; MSPB 1996.

41. *Board of County Commissioners v. Umbehr*, 135 L.Ed.2d 843 (1996); *O'Hare Truck Service v. Northlake*, 135 L.Ed.2d 874 (1996).

BIBLIOGRAPHY

Aberbach, Joel D., & Bert A. Rockman. 1976. "Clashing Beliefs Within the Executive Branch: The Nixon Administration Bureaucracy." *American Political Science Review*. 70:2, pp. 456-468.

Abramson, Paul R., John H. Aldrich, and David W. Rohde. 1995. *Change and Continuity in the 1992 Elections*. Washington: Congressional Quarterly.

Arnold, Peri. 1986. *Making the Managerial Presidency*. Princeton: Princeton University Press.

Aron, Cindy Sondik. 1989. *Ladies and Gentlemen of the Civil Service: Middle-Class Workers in Victorian America*. New York: Oxford University Press.

Aronson, Sidney H. 1964. *Status and Kinship in the Higher Civil Service: Standards of Selection in the Administrations of John Adams, Thomas Jefferson, and Andrew Jackson*. Cambridge: Harvard University Press.

Bailyn, Bernard. 1977. *The Ideological Origins of the American Revolution*. Cambridge: Harvard University Press.

Ban, Carolyn, & Patricia W. Ingraham. 1988. "Retaining Quality Federal Employees: Life After PACE." *Public Administration Review*. 48:3, pp. 708-718.

Ban, Carolyn. 1995. *How Do Public Managers Manage? Bureaucratic Constraints, Organizational Culture, and the Potential For Reform*. San Francisco: Jossey-Bass.

Barnes, James A. 1989. "Changing Company Town." *National Journal*. February 4, pp. 278-282.

Barr, Stephen. 1996. "'Un-Hatched' Workers Practice Their Politics." *Washington Post*." August 26, p. A11.

Barr, Stephen. 1997. "Union Criticized for 'Witch Hunt.'" *Washington Post*. January 3, p. A19.

Barr, Stephen. 1993. "Bureaucracy Review Opens with a Rally."*Washington Post.* April 16, p. A23.

Barzelay, Michael, with Babak J. Armajani. 1992. *Breaking Through Bureaucracy: A New Vision For Managing in Government.* Berkeley: University of California Press.

Bennis, Warren G., & Phillip E. Slater. 1968. *The Temporary Society.* New York: Harper & Row.

Bernstein, Marver. 1958. *The Job of the Federal Executive.* Washington: Brookings.

Bonafede, Dom. 1981. "Reagan and His Kitchen Cabinet are Bound by Friendship and Ideology." *National Journal.* 13:5, pp. 608-613.

Bonafede, Dom. 1981b. "New Right Preaches a New Religion, and Ronald Reagan Is Its Prophet," *National Journal.* 13:19, pp. 779-783.

Bonafede, Donald. 1987. "The White House Personnel Office from Roosevelt to Reagan." In G. Calvin Mackenzie ed., *The In-and-Outers.* Baltimore: Johns Hopkins University Press, pp. 30-59.

Brauer, Carl M. 1986. *Presidential Transitions: Eisenhower Through Reagan.* New York: Oxford University Press.

Brownlow, Louis, Charles E. Merriam, and Luther Gulick. 1978"Report of the President's Committee on Administrative Management." In Harry A. Bailey, ed., *Classics of the American Presidency.* Oak Park, IL: Moore, pp. 126-130.

Brownstein, Ronald, and Nina Easton. 1983. *Reagan's Ruling Class.* New York: Pantheon.

Burnham, Walter Dean. 1970. *Critical Elections and the Mainstream of American Politics.* New York: W.W. Norton.

Burns, James MacGregor. 1985. *The American Experiment: The Workshop of Democracy.* New York: Alfred Knopf.

Callow, Alexander. 1965. *The Tweed Ring.* London: Oxford University Press.

Carter, Stephen L. 1994. *The Confirmation Mess: Cleaning Up the Federal Appointment Process.* New York: Basic Books.

Census Bureau, U.S. Department of Commerce. 1989. *Statistical Abstract of the United States: 1989.* Washington, D.C.:

Government Printing Office.

Census Bureau, U.S. Department of Commerce. 1971. *Historical Statistics of the United States: Colonial Times to 1970.* Washington, D.C.: Government Printing Office.

Census Bureau, U.S. Department of Commerce. 1988. *Statistical Abstract of the United States: 1988.* Washington, D.C.: Government Printing Office.

Clark, Peter B. 1961. "Incentive Systems: A Theory of Organizations." *Administrative Science Quarterly.* 6:2, pp. 129-166.

Clinton, Bill and Al Gore. 1992. *Putting People First.* New York: Times Books.

Cole, Richard L., & David A. Caputo. 1979. "Presidential Control of the Senior Civil Service: Assessing the Strategies of the Nixon Years." *American Political Science Review.* 73:2, pp. 399-413.

Cook, Brian J. 1996. *Bureaucracy and Self-Government: Reconsidering the Role of Public Administation in American Politics.* Baltimore: The Johns Hopkins University Press.

Dahl, Robert. 1965. *A Preface to Democratic Theory.* Chicago: University of Chicago Press.

Devine, Donald J. 1985. *Public Administration in the Reagan Era.* Washington: Office of Personnel Management.

Devroy, Ann. 1989. "Political Gaffe Seen in Census Hiring,"*Washington Post.* October 24, p. A5.

Dionne, E.J., Jr. 1991. *Why Americans Hate Politics.* New York: Simon & Schuster.

Doud, Maureen. 1990. "President Vetos a Bill and Makes Threat on Second." *New York Times.* June 16, p. A1.

Downs, Anthony. 1966. *Inside Bureaucracy.* Boston: Little, Brown.

Downs, Fred., 1987. "It's Time West Point Stopped Sugarcoating Combat." *Washington Post National Weekly Edition.* August 31, pp. 23-24.

Dulles, Foster Rhea. 1964. *Labor in America: A History.* New York: Thomas Y. Crowell.

Dunlop, Becky Norton. 1987. "The Role of the White House Office of Personnel." In Robert Rector & Michael Sanera, ed., *Steering the Elephant: How Washington Really Works*. New York: Universe Books, pp. 145-155.

Durant, Robert F. 1992. *The Administrative Presidency Revisited: Public Lands, the BLM, and the Reagan Revolution*. Albany: State University of New York Press.

Edwards, David. 1988. *The American Political Experience: An Introduction to Government*. Englewood Cliffs: Prentice Hall.

Elazar, Daniel J. 1972. *American Federalism: A View from the States*. New York: Harper & Row.

Epstein, Leon D. 1982. *Political Parties in Western Democracies*. New Brunswick: Transaction Books.

Fallows, James. 1979. "The Passionless Presidency," *Atlantic*. 245, pp. 33-48.

Fallows, James. 1979. "The Passionless Presidency II," *Atlantic*. 246, pp. 75-81.

Fenno, Richard J. 1959. *The President's Cabinet*. Cambridge: Harvard University Press.

Fesler, James W. 1975. "Public Administration and the Social Sciences: 1946 to 1960." In Frederick C. Mosher, ed., *American Public Administration: Past, Present, Future*. University, AL: University of Alabama Press, pp. 97-141.

Fiorina, Morris P. 1977. *Congress: Keystone of the Washington Establishment*. New Haven: Yale University Press.

Frederickson, H. George. 1989. "Minnowbrook II: Changing Epochs of Public Administration." *Public Administration Review*. 49:2, pp. 97-103.

Frederickson, H. George. 1978. "Toward a New Public Administration." In Jay M. Shafritz and Albert C. Hyde, eds., *Classics of Public Administration*. Oak Park: Moore, pp. 391-404.

Friedman, Milton. 1983. "Sticking Price Tags on Job Performance in Government." *Management*. August, 4, pp. 10-12.

GAO. 1992. *Political Appointees: Turnover Rates in Executive Schedule Positions Requiring Senate Confirmation*. Washington: Government Printing Office.

GAO. 1982. *Effects of the Presidential Transition on the SES*. Letter to Representative Patricia Schroeder.

Garvey, Gerald. 1993. *Facing the Bureaucracy*. San Francisco: Jossey-Bass.

Germond, Jack W. and Jules Witcover. 1989. "Reaganites Worry About Fading of Reaganism." *National Journal*. January 7, p. 35.

Gerth, H.H., C. Wright Mills, eds., 1979. *From Max Weber: Essays in Sociology*. New York: Oxford University Press.

Ginsberg, Benjamin and Martin Shefter. 1990. *Politics by Other Means*. New York: Basic Books.

Goodnow, Frank. 1967. *Politics and Administration*. New York: Russell & Russell.

Goodsell, Charles T. 1994. *The Case for Bureaucracy*. Chatham, NJ: Chatham House.

Goodsell, Charles T. 1985. *The Case for Bureaucracy*. Chatham, NJ: Chatham House.

Goodsell, Charles T. 1984. "The Grace Commission: Seeking Efficiency for the Whole People?" *Public Administration Review*. 44:3, pp. 196-204.

Goodwin, Lawrence. 1978. *The Populist Movement*. New York: Oxford University Press.

Gore, Al. 1994. *The Gore Report on Reinventing Government*. New York: Random House.

Gore Al. 1993. *The Gore Report on Reinventing Government*. New York: Random House.

Gore, Al. 1995. *Common Sense Government*. New York: Random House.

Greenstein, Fred I. 1982. *The Hidden-Hand Presidency: Eisenhower as Leader*. New York: Basic.

Gugliotta, Guy. 1996. "Total Management, Little Quality." *Washington Post*. December 3, A13.

Guy, Mary Ellen. 1989. "Minnowbrook II: Conclusions." *Public Administration Review*. 49:2, pp. 219-220.

Hammer, Michael, & James Champy. 1993. *Reengineering the Corporation: A Manifesto for Business Revolution*. New York: HarperCollins.

Harrington, Michael. 1962. *The Other America: Poverty in the*

United States. New York: Penguin Books.

Harris, Fred R. 1986. *American Democracy: The Ideal and the Reality*. Glenview: Scott, Foresman and Company.

Haveman, Judith. 1989. "Senior Civil Servants Face New Rules with Pay Hike." *Washington Post*. October 21, A8.

Heclo, Hugh. 1975. "The OMB and the Presidency—The Problem of Neutral Competence." *The Public Interest*. 78, pp. 80-98.

Heclo, Hugh, & Lester M. Salamon eds., 1981. *The Illusion of Presidential Government*. Boulder: Westview.

Heclo, Hugh. 1977. *A Government of Strangers*. Washington: Brookings.

Hess, Stephen. 1976. *Organizing the Presidency*. Washington: Brookings.

Hibbing, John R., & Elizabeth Theiss-Morse. 1995. *Congress as Public Enemy: Public Attitudes Toward American Political Institution*. New York: Cambridge University Press.

Hinkley, Barbara & Sheldon Goldman. 1990. *American Politics and Government: Structure, Process, Institutions, and Policies*. Glenview: Scott Foresman and Company.

Hodgson, Godfrey. 1978. *America in Our Time: From World War II to Nixon, What Happened and Why*. New York: Vintage Books.

Hofstadter, Richard. 1964. *Anti-Intellectualism in American Life*. New York: Vintage.

Hofstadter, Richard. 1989. *The American Political Tradition and the Men Who Made It*. New York: Vintage Books.

Hofstadter, Richard. 1955. *The Age of Reform*. New York: Vintage.

Hoogenboom, Ari. 1961. *Outlawing the Spoils*. Urbana: University of Illinois Press.

Horner, Constance. 1994. "Deregulating the Federal Service: Is the Time Right?." In John J. DiIulio, Jr., ed., *Deregulating the Public Service: Can Government Be Improved?*. Washington: Brookings, pp. 85-101.

Howard, Philip K. 1994. *The Death of Common Sense: How Law Is Suffocating America*. New York: Random House.

Huberty, Robert M., & James L. Malone. 1981. "The Senior Executive Service." In Chalres L. Heatherly, eds., *Mandate for*

Leadership. Washington, D.C. Heritage Foundation, pp. 869-901.

Huddleston, Mark W. 1987. *The Government's Managers*. New York: Priority Press.

Hult, Karen M., and Charles Walcott. 1990. *Governing Public Organizations: Politics, Structures, and Institutional Design*. Belmont: Wadsworth.

Hurd, Richard W., & Jill K. Kriesky. 1985. " 'The Rise and Demise of PATCO' Reconstructed," *Industrial and Labor Relations Review*. 40:1, pp. 115-120.

Ingraham, Patricia Wallace. 1995. *The Foundation of Merit: Public Service in American Democracy*. Baltimore: The Johns Hopkins University Press.

Ingraham, Patricia Wallace, & David H. Rosenbloom. 1989. "The New Public Personnel and the New Public Service." *Public Administration Review*. 49:2, pp. 118-126.

Ingraham, Patricia Wallace. 1987. "Applying Models of Political-Career Relationships to Policy Implementation." Unpublished paper presented at the annual American Political Science Association Convention, Chicago, Illinois.

Ingraham, Patricia Wallace. 1987b. "Building Bridges or Destroying Them: The President, the Appointees, and the Bureaucracy." *Public Administration Review*. 47:5, pp. 425-435.

Ingraham, Patricia Wallace, & Carolyn R. Ban. 1986. "Models of Public Management: Are They Useful to Federal Managers in the 1980's?" *Public Administration Review*. 46:2, pp. 152-160.

Ingraham, Patricia Wallace & C. Barrilleaux. 1983. "Motivating Government Managers for Retrenchment: Some Possible Lessons from the Senior Executive Service." *Public Administration Review*. 43:5, pp. 393-402.

Ingraham, Patricia Wallace, & Carolyn R. Ban., eds., 1984. *Legislating Bureaucratic Change: The Civil Service Reform Act of 1978*. Albany: State University of New York Press.

Ingraham, Patricia Wallace, James R. Thompson, & Elliot F. Eisenberg. 1995. "Political Management Strategies and Political/Career Relationships: Where Are We Now in the Federal Government?" *Public Administration Review*. May June. 55:3;

pp. 263-272.

Jacobson, Gary C. 1983. *The Politics of Congressional Elections.* Boston: Little, Brown.

Kane, Brian. 1990. "Post Office Privitization Comes to Binghamton, N.Y." *Labor Notes.* July, p. 3.

Kaufman, Herbert. 1976. *Are Government Organizations Immortal?* Washington: Brookings.

Kaufman, Herbert. 1973. *Administrative Feedback: Monitoring Subordinates' Behavior.* Washington: Brookings.

Kaufman, Herbert. 1981. *The Administrative Behavior of Federal Bureau Chiefs.* Washington: Brookings.

Kaufman, Herbert. 1971. *The Limits of Organizational Change.* University, AL: University of Alabama Press.

Kaufman, Herbert. 1967. *The Forest Ranger.* Baltimore: Johns Hopkins University Press.

Kaufman, Herbert. 1956. "Emerging Conflicts in the Doctrines of Public Administration." *American Political Science Review.* 50:4, pp. 1057-1073.

Kettl, Donald F., Patricia W. Ingraham, Ronald P. Sanders, and Constance Horner. 1996. *Civil Service Reform: Building a Government That Works.* Washington: Brookings.

Kettl, Donald F. & John J. DiIulio, Jr., ed., 1995. *Inside the Reinvention Machine: Appraising Governmental Reform.* Washington: Brookings.

King, Desmond. 1995. *Separate and Unequal: Black Americans and the United States Federal Government.* New York: Oxford University Press.

Kirschten, Dick. 1981. "You Say You Want a Subcabinet Post? Clear It with Marty, Dick, Lyn, or Fred.," *National Journal.* April 4, pp. 564-567.

Kirschten, Dick. 1980. "Wanted: 275 Reagan Team Players; Empire Builders Need Not Apply." *National Journal.* December 6, pp. 2077-2079.

Kirschten, Dick. 1983. "Administration Using Carter-Era Reform to Manipulate the Levers of Government." *National Journal.* April 9, pp. 732-736.

Knott, Jack H. & Gary J. Miller. 1987. *Reforming Bureaucracy*. Englewood Cliffs, NJ: Prentice Hall.

Krislov, Samuel & David H. Rosenbloom. 1981. *Representative Bureaucracy and the American Political System*. New York: Praeger.

Leuchtenburg, William E. 1963. *Franklin D. Roosevelt and the New Deal*. New York: Harper & Row.

Levitan, Sar A. & Robert Taggart. 1976. *The Promise of Greatness*. Cambridge: Harvard University Press.

Levitan, Sar A. & Alexandra B. Nodeen. 1983. *Working for the Sovereign: Employee Relations in the Federal Government*. Baltimore: Johns Hopkins Press.

Levy, Leonard. 1988. *Original Intent and the Framers' Constitution*. New York: MacMillan Publishing.

Lewis, Gregory B. 1988. "Progress Toward Racial and Sexual Equality in the Federal Service." *Public Administration Review*. 48:3, pp. 701-710.

Light, Paul C. 1987. "When Worlds Collide: The Political-Career Nexis." In G. Calvin Mackenzie, ed., *The In-and-Outers*. Baltimore: Johns Hopkins University Press, pp. 156-173.

Long, Norton E. 1949. "Power and Administration." *Public Administration Review*. 9, pp. 257-264.

Lowery, David & Caryl E. Rusbult. 1986. "Bureaucratic Responses to Antibureaucratic Administrations." *Administration and Society*. 18:1; pp. 45-75.

Lowi, Theodore J. 1979. *The End of Liberalism*. New York: Norton.

Lowi, Theodore J. 1985. *The Personal President*. Ithaca: Cornell University Press.

Mackenzie, G. Calvin, ed. 1987., *The In-and-Outers*. Baltimore: Johns Hopkins University Press.

Mackenzie, G. Calvin and Robert Shogan. 1996. *Obstacle Course*. New York: Twentieth Century Fund.

Mackenzie, G. Calvin. 1981. *The Politics of Presidential Appointments*. New York: Free Press.

Madison, James, et al. 1937. *The Federalist*. New York: The Modern Library.

Malone, Dumas & Basil Rauch. 1960. *Empire for Liberty: The Genesis and Growth of the United States of America,* volume II. New York: Appleton-Century Crofts.

Maranto, Robert. 1993b. *Politics and Bureaucracy in the Modern Presidency.* Westport, CT: Greenwood.

Maranto, Robert. 1994. "Reinventing All Over Again: The Clinton Transition in the Civil Service." Unpublished paper presented at the annual American Political Science Association meeting, New York City.

Maranto, Robert. 1993. "Exploring the Clinton Transition: Views From the Career Civil Service." Unpublished paper presented at the annual American Political Science Association meeting, Washington, D.C.

Maranto, Robert. 1995. "Comparing the Clinton, Bush, and Reagan Transitions in the Bureaucracy: Views from the Bureaucrats." Unpublished paper presented at the annual Midwest Political Science Association meeting, Chicago, Illinois.

Maranto, Robert. 1996. Thinking the Unthinkable in Public Administration: a Case for Spoils. Unpublished paper.

Maranto, Robert & David Schultz. 1991. *A Short History of the United States Civil Service.* Lanham, Maryland: University Press of America.

Marshall, Will & Martin Schram, eds., 1993. *Mandate for Leadership.* New York: Berkley Books.

Masters, Marick F. 1985. "Federal-Employee Unions and Political Action." *Industrial and Labor Relations Review.* 38:4, pp. 612-620.

Mayhew, David R. 1974. *Congress: The Electoral Connection.* New Haven: Yale University Press.

McConnell, Grant. 1966. *Private Power and American Democracy.* New York: Vintage Books.

McGregor, Douglas Murray. 1978. "The Human Side of Enterprise."In Jay M. Shafritz & Albert C. Hyde, eds., *Classics of Public Administration.* Oak Park, IL: Moore, pp. 187-193.

Meacham, John. 1993. "What Al Gore Might Learn the Hard Way." *Washington Monthly.* September 16-20, p. A1.

Medeiros, James A. and Schmitt, David E. 1977. *Public Bureaucracy: Values and Perspectives*. North Scituate, Massachusetts: Duxbury Press.

Merit System Protection Board. 1996. *Fair and Equitable Treatment: A Progress Report on Minority Employment in the Federal Government*. Washington, D.C.

Merit System Protection Board. 1983. *Reduction in Force in the Federal Government: What Happened and the Opportunities for Improvement*. Washington, D.C.

Milward, H. Brinton. 1995. "Implications of Contracting out: New Roles for the Hollow State." In Patricia Wallace Ingraham and Barbara Romzek, eds., *New Paradigms for Government: Issues for the Changing Public Service*. San Francisco: Jossey-Bass, pp. 41-62.

Mosher, Frederick C. 1982. *Democracy and the Public Service*. New York: Oxford University Press.

Mosher, Frederick. 1984. *A Tale of Two Agencies*. Baton Rouge: LSU Press.

Mosher, Lawrence. 1983. "Ruckelshaus Is Seen as His Own Man In Battle to Renew Clean Water Act." *National Journal*. 15:29, pp. 1497-1500.

Moynihan, Daniel P. 1969. *Maximum Feasible Misunderstanding*. New York: The Free Press.

Murphy, Thomas P., Donald E. Nuechterlein, and Ronald J. Stupak. 1978. *Inside the Bureaucracy: The View From the Assistant Secretary's Desk*. Boulder: Westview.

Nathan, Richard. 1983. *The Administrative Presidency*. New York: John Wiley.

Nathan, Richard P. 1985. "Political Administration Is Legitimate." In in Lester M. Salamon and Michael S. Lund, eds., *The Reagan Presidency and the Governing of America*. Washington: Urban Institute Press, pp. 375-380.

National Journal. 1989. "A Gathering of Friends." June 10, pp. 1402-1403.

Nelson, Michael, ed., 1993. *The Elections of 1992*. Washington, D.C.: CQ Press.

Nelson, Michael. 1982. "A Short, Ironic History of American National Bureaucracy." *Journal of Politics.* 44:2, pp. 747-778.

Nelson, William E. 1982. *The Roots of American Bureaucracy.* Cambridge: Harvard University Press.

Newland, Chester A. 1983. "A Mid-Term Appraisal—The Reagan Presidency: Limited Government and Political Administration." *Public Administration Review.* 43:1, pp. 1-21.

Niskanen, William A., Jr. 1971. *Bureaucracy and Representative Government.* Chicago: Aldine-Atherton.

Northrup, Herbert R. and Amie D. Thorton. 1985. *The Federal Government as Employer: The Federal Labor Relations Authority and the PATCO Challenge.* Philadelphia: The Wharton School of the University of Pennsylvania.

O'Connor, David. 1993. "Reinventing Government: Creating an Entrepreneurial Federal Establishment." In Will Marshall and Martin Schram eds., *Mandate For Leadership.* New York: Berkley Books, pp. 263-187.

O'Connor, Edwin. 1956. *The Last Hurrah.* Boston: Little, Brown and Company.

Osborne, David, and Ted Gaebler. 1992. *Reinventing Government: How the Entrepreneurial Spirit Is Transforming the Public Sector.* Reading, Massachusetts: Addison-Wesley.

Ostrom, Vincent. 1974. *The Intellectual Crisis in American Public Administration.* University, AL: University of Alabama Press.

Pessen, Edward. 1978. *Jacksonian America: Society, Personality, and Politics.* Homeswood: Dorsey Press.

Pessen, Edward. 1984. *The Log Cabin Myth.* New Haven: Yale University Press.

Peters, Charles. 1992. *How Washington Really Works.* Reading: Addison-Wesley.

Peters, Charles. 1978. "A Kind Word for the Spoils System." In Charles Peters & Michael Nelson, ed., *The Culture of Bureaucracy.* New York: Holt, Rinehart & Winston, pp. 263-267.

Peters, Thomas J., 1989. *Thriving on Chaos: Handbook for a Management Revolution.* New York: Harper and Row.

Peters, Thomas J. and Robert H. Waterman, Jr. 1982. *In Search of*

Excellence: Lessons From America's Best Run Companies. New York: Warner.

Pfiffner, James P. 1987. "Political Appointees and Career Executives: The Democracy-Bureaucracy Nexis in the Third Century." *Public Administration Review.* 47:1, pp. 57-65.

Pfiffner, James P. 1985. "Political Public Administration." *Public Administration Review.* 45:2, pp. 352-356.

Pfiffner, James P. 1990. "Establishing the Bush Presidency." *Public Administration Review.* 50:1: pp. 64-73.

Pfiffner, James P. 1988. *The Strategic Presidency.* Chicago: Dorsey.

Pfiffner, James P. 1996. *The Strategic Presidency: Hitting the Ground Running.* Lawrence: University of Kansas Press.

Pincus, Ann. 1978. "How to Get a Government Job." In Charles Peters and Michael Nelson, eds., *The Culture of Bureaucracy.* 1978. New York: Holt, Rinehart, and Winston, pp. 188-192.

Pitkin, Hanna Fenichel. 1972. *The Concept of Representation.* Berkeley: University of California Press.

Plowden, William. 1984. "The Higher Civil Service of Britain." In Bruce L.R. Smith ed., *The Higher Civil Service in Europe and Canada.* Washington, D.C.: Brookings, pp. 20-39.

Podhoretz, John. 1993. *Hell of a Ride: Backstage at the White House Follies, 1989-1993.* New York: Simon and Schuster.

Podhoretz, John. 1993. *Hell of a Ride.* New York: Simon and Schuster.

Pomper, Gerald, et al. 1981. *The Election of 1980: Reports and Interpretations.* Chatham, NJ: Chatham House.

Popkin Samuel L. 1994. *The Reasoning Voter: Communication and Persuasion in Presidential Campaigns.* Chicago: University of Chicago Press.

Rackove, Jack N. 1996. "The Original Intention of Original Understanding." *Constitutional Commentary.* 13:2, pp. 159-170.

Ranney, Austin. 1981. *The American Elections of 1980.* Washington, D.C.: American Enterprise Institute.

Raybeck, Joesph G. 1966. *A History of American Labor.* New York: The Free Press.

Riordon, William L. 1963. *Plunkett of Tammany Hall.* New York:

Dutton.

Ripley, Randall B. & Grace A. Franklin. 1976. *Congress, the Bureaucracy, and Public Policy*. Homewood: Dorsey.

Roberts, Paul Craig. 1984. *The Supply-Side Revolution*. Cambridge: Harvard University Press.

Rockman, Bert A. 1991. "The Leadership Style of George Bush." In Colin Campbell and Rockman, eds., *The Bush Presidency: First Appraisals*. Chatham, NJ: Chatham House, pp. 1-36.

Romzek, Barbara S. 1985. "The Effects of Public Service Recognition, Job Security, and Staff Reductions on Organizational Involvement." *Public Administration Review*. 45:2, pp. 282-291.

Rosen, Bernard. 1982. *Holding Government Accountable*. New York: Praeger.

Rosen, Bernard. 1981. "Uncertainty in the Senior Executive Service."*Public Adminstration Review*. 41:2, 203-207.

Rosenberg, Charles E. 1968. *The Trial of the Assassin Guiteau*. Chicago: University of Chicago Press.

Rosenbloom, David H. 1982. "Politics and Public Personnel Administration." In David H. Rosenbloom, ed., *Centenary Issues of the Pendleton Act of 1883*. New York: Marcel Dekker, pp. 1-10.

Rosenbloom, David H. 1983. *Public Administration and Law: Bench v. Bureau in the United States*. New York: Marcel Dekker, Inc.

Rosenbloom, David H. 1971. *Federal Service and the Constitution: The Development of the Public Employment Relationship*. Ithaca, New York: Cornell University Press.

Rubin, Irene S. 1985. *Shrinking the Federal Government*. New York: Longman.

Sanera, Michael. 1987. "Paradoxical Lessons from *In Search of Excellence*." In Rector, Robert & Michael Sanera, eds., *Steering the Elephant: How Washington Really Works*. New York: Universe Books, pp. 163-169.

Sanera, Michael. 1984. "Implementing the Mandate." In Stuart M. Butler, Michael Sanera, and W. Bruce Weinrod eds., *Mandate For Leadership II*. Washington, D.C.: Heritage Foundation, pp.

457-560.

Savas E.S. & Sigmund G. Ginsburg. 1973. "The Civil Service: A Meritless System?." *The Public Interest*. 32, pp. 70-85.

Savas, E.S. 1987. *Privatization: the Key to Better Government*. Chatham, NJ: Chatham House.

Savas E.S. 1982. *Privatizing the Public Sector*. Chatham, NJ: Chatham House.

Schiesl, Martin. 1977. *The Politics of Efficiency*. Berkeley: University of California Press.

Schlesinger, Arthur, Jr. 1957. *The Crisis of the Old Order*. Boston: Houghton Mifflin Company.

Sellers, Charles. 1991. *The Market Revolution: Jacksonian America, 1815-1846*. New York: Oxford University Press.

Shoop, Tom. 1993. Goring the Bureaucracy. *Government Executive* October, pp. 12-16.

Skocpol, Theda. 1992. *Protecting Soldiers and Mothers: The Political Origins of Social Welfare Policy in the United States*. Cambridge, MA: Belknap Press.

Skrowronek Stephen. 1982, *Building a New American State: The Expansion of National Administrative Capacities, 1877-1920*. New York: Cambridge University Press.

Solomon, Burt. 1989. "SubCabinet: A Mix of Expert...the Untried and the Well Connected.," *National Journal*. April 29, pp. 1056-1057.

Solomon, Burt A. 1993. "To Win a Big Job With Clinton...Pull, But Please Don't Push." *National Journal*. January 30, pp. 300-301.

Somers, Herman Miles. 1954. "The Federal Bureaucracy and the Change of Administrations." *American Political Science Review*. 48:1. pp. 131-151.

Stillman, Richard J. II. 1987. *The American Bureaucracy*. Chicago: Nelson-Hall.

Stone, Alice B. & Donald C. Stone. 1975. "Early Development of Education in Public Administration." In Frederick C. Mosher ed.,, *American Public Administration: Past, Present, Future*. University, AL: University of Alabama Press, pp. 1-10.

Taylor, Frederick. 1911. *The Principles of Scientific Management*.

New York: W.W. Norton & Company.

Thompson, Victor A. 1982. *Without Sympathy or Enthusiasm: The Problem of Administrative Compassion.* University: University of Alabama Press.

United States Merit System Protection Board. 1983. "Reduction-in-Force in the Federal Government, 1981." Washington, D.C.

Uslaner, Eric M. 1993. *The Decline of Comity in Congress.* Ann Arbor: University of Michigan Press.

Van Riper, Paul P. 1983. "The American Administrative State: Wilson and the Founders—An Unorthodox View." *Public Administration Review.* 43:6, pp. 477-490.

Van Riper, Paul P. 1958. *History of the United States Civil Service.* Evanston, IL: Row, Peterson & Company.

Waldo, Dwight. 1978. "Public Administration in a Time of Revolution." In Jay M. Shafritz and Albert C. Hyde, eds., *Classics of Public Administration.* Oak Park, IL: Moore, pp. 170-182.

Walker, Wallace Earl & Michael R. Reopel. 1986. "Strategies for Governance: Transition and Domestic Policymaking in the Reagan Administration." *Presidential Studies Quarterly.* 16:4, pp. 734-760.

Weko, Thomas J. 1995. *The Politicized Presidency: The White House Personnel Office, 1948-1994.* Lawrence: University Press of Kansas.

Williams, Walter. 1990. *Mismanaging America: The Rise of the Anti-Analytic Presidency.* Lawrence: University Press of Kansas.

Wilson, James Q. 1968. *Varieties of Police Behavior.* Cambridge: Harvard University Press.

Wilson, James Q. 1973. *Political Organizations.* New York: Basic.

Wilson, Graham K. 1980. "Are Department Secretaries Really a President's Natural Enemies?" In Harry A. Bailey, Jr., ed.,, *Classics of the American Presidency.* Oak Park, IL: Moore, pp. 134-150.

Wilson, Woodrow. 1968b. "Notes on Administration," in *The Papers of Woodrow Wilson*, volume 5, Arthur Link. ed.,, Princeton: Princeton University Press, pp. 49-55.

Wilson, Woodrow. 1968a. "The Study of Administration," in *The Papers of Woodrow,* volume 5, Arthur Link, ed.,, Princeton: Princeton University Press, pp. 359-380.

Wilson, James Q. 1976. "The Rise of the Bureaucratic State," in *The American Commonwealth*. Nathan Galzer & Irving Kristol eds., New York: Basic, pp. 77-103.

Wilson, James Q. 1986. *American Government: Institutions and Policies*. Lexington, MA: D.C. Heath.

Cases

Barenblatt v. United States, 360 U.S. 109 (1959).
Board of County Commissioners v. Umbehr, 135 L.Ed.2d 843 (1996).
Branti v. Finkel, 445 U.S.507 (1980).
Carter v. Carter Coal Company, 298 U.S. 238 (1936)
Dennis v. United States, 341 U.S. 494 (1951).
Dole v. United Steelworkers of America, 494 U.S. 26 (1990).
Douglas v. Hampton, 512 F.2d 976 (D.C.Cir. 1975).
Elrod v. Burns, 427 U.S. 347 (1976).
Ex parte Curtis, 106 U.S. 371 (1882).
Goldberg v. Kelly, 397 U.S. 254 (1970).
Hoke v. Henderson, 15 N.C. 1 (1833).
Humphrey's Executor v. United States, 292 U.S. 602 (1935).
Luevano v. Campbell, 93 F.R.D. 68 (1981).
Marbury v. Madison, 5 U.S. 137 (1803).
McAuliffe v. New Bedford, 155 Mass. 216 (1892).
Meyers v. United States, 272 U.S. 52 (1926).
Morrison v. Olson, 487 U.S. 654 (1988).
Mulford v. Smith, 307 U.S. 39 (1939).
National Treasury Employees Union v. Von Raab, 489 U.S. 656
      (1989).
.NLRB v. Jones & McLaughlin Steel, 301 U.S. 1 (1937).
O'Hare Truck Service v. Northlake, 135 L.Ed.2d 874 (1996).
Panama Refining Company v. Ryan, 293 U.S. 388 (1935).
Perry v. Sindermann, 408 U.S. 593 (1972).
Rutan v. Republican Party of Illinois, 497 U.S. 62 (1990)
Schechter Poultry v. United States, 295 U.S. 495 (1935).
Skinner v. Railway Labor Executives Association, 489 U.S. 602
      (1989).
United States v. Darby, 312 U.S. 100 (1940).

United States v. Nixon, 418, U.S. 683 (1974).

United Public Workers v. Mitchell, 330 U.S. 75 (1947).

United States Civil Service Commission v. National Association of Letter Carriers, 413 U.S. 548 (1972).

United States v. Wurzbach, 108 U.S. 397 (1929).

Watkins v. United States, 354 U.S. 178 (1957).

Wickard v. Filburn, 317 U.S. 111 (1942).

Yakus v. United States, 421 U.S. 414 (1944).

Index

242

174, 188.

Office of Personnel Management
(OPM), 151, 171, 210.

Office of Price Administration
(OPA), 114.

Office of Production Management
(OPM), 114.

*O'Hare Truck Service v. City of
Northlake*, 214, 217.

Osborne, David, 207.

Panama Refining Company v. Ryan,
106.

Paperwork Reduction Act of 1980,
174, 178.

Patent Office, 39.

Pendleton, George, 62, 63, 66, 73, 79.

Pendleton Act, 20, 49, 60, 63, 64, 65,
66, 73, 87, 94.

Performance Rating Act of 1950,
128.

Perot, Ross, 198.

Perry v. Sindermann, 143.

Peters, Charles, 206-207.

Pierce, Franklin, 43.

Plunkett, George, 41, 56, 57, 83.

Politics/Administration Dichotomy,
8, 10-12, 63-64, 73, 75-82, 82-
83, 183, 185, 213-214.

Populists, 3, 74.

Presidential removal power, 25, 26,
27, 28, 29, 34, 50, 53, 107.

Privatization, 192, 207, 210-212.

Professional and Clerical
Examinations (PACE), 134, 156.

Progressives, 82-84, 85, 90.

Public Works Administration (PWA),
105.

Public Air Traffic Controllers
(PATCO), 117, 172-174.

Radical Republicans, 54.

Ramspeck Acts of 1938,1940,1943,

Reagan, Ronald, 2, 5,, 12, 135, 151-

152, 161-178, 184, 186.

Reconstruction Finance Corporation
(RFC), 103, 127.

Reed, Stanley, 111.

Reinventing Government, 207, 208-
212.

Representation, 23, 25, 39-41, 63-66,
155-156.

Revolutionary War, 21-26.

Riley, Richard, 201.

Roosevelt, Franklin, 74, 101-115.

Roosevelt, Theodore, 59, 82-83, 88,
89-90, 92.

Rutan v. Republican Party of Illinois,
159, 178.

Rutledge, Wiley, 111.

Schechter Poultry v. U.S, 106, 107.

Schurz, Carl, 87.

Scientific Management, 84-87, see
also Taylorism.

Securities and Exchange Commission
(SEC), 105.

Senior Executive Service (SES), 150-
152, 161, 167-172, 176, 184,
185, 190.

Separation of powers, 5, 8, 9-10, 12-
13, 28, 34, 53, 106-107.

Seward, William, 53.

Skinner v. Transportation Workers,
174, 181.

Spoils (patronage), 2, 6, 8, 9, 10, 14,
20, 28-29, 33, 35-40, 42, 43, 44,
45, 49, 50, 51, 54, 63-66, 74,
105, 110, 111, 112, 124, 151,
152-155, 178, 214.

Subgovernments, 89.

Sumner, Charles, 51.

Swartout, Samuel, 41.

Taft, William H., 90-91, 92, 107.

Taft-Hartley Act, 117.

Tammany Hall, 41, 56, 57.

Taylor, Frederick (Taylorism), 84-87,

Teaching Texts in Law and Politics

David Schultz, *General Editor*

The new series Teaching Texts in Law and Politics is devoted to textbooks that explore the multidimensional and multidisciplinary areas of law and politics. Special emphasis will be given to textbooks written for the undergraduate classroom. Subject matters to be addressed in this series include, but will not be limited to: constitutional law; civil rights and liberties issues; law, race, gender, and gender orientation studies; law and ethics; women and the law; judicial behavior and decision-making; legal theory; comparative legal systems; criminal justice; courts and the political process; and other topics on the law and the political process that would be of interest to undergraduate curriculum and education. Submission of single-author and collaborative studies, as well as collections of essays are invited.

Authors wishing to have works considered for this series should contact:

Peter Lang Publishing
Acquisitions Department
275 Seventh Avenue, 28th floor
New York, New York 10001